SpringerBriefs in Sociology

SpringerBriefs in Sociology are concise summaries of cutting-edge research and practical applications across the field of sociology. These compact monographs are refereed by and under the editorial supervision of scholars in Sociology or cognate fields. Volumes are 50 to 125 pages (approximately 20,000- 70,000 words), with a clear focus. The series covers a range of content from professional to academic such as snapshots of hot and/or emerging topics, in-depth case studies, and timely reports of state-of-the art analytical techniques. The scope of the series spans the entire field of Sociology, with a view to significantly advance research. The character of the series is international and multi-disciplinary and will include research areas such as: health, medical, intervention studies, cross-cultural studies, race/class/gender, children, youth, education, work and organizational issues, relationships, religion, ageing, violence, inequality, critical theory, culture, political sociology, social psychology, and so on. Volumes in the series may analyze past, present and/or future trends, as well as their determinants and consequences. Both solicited and unsolicited manuscripts are considered for publication in this series. SpringerBriefs in Sociology will be of interest to a wide range of individuals, including sociologists, psychologists, economists, philosophers, health researchers, as well as practitioners across the social sciences. Briefs will be published as part of Springer's eBook collection, with millions of users worldwide. In addition, Briefs will be available for individual print and electronic purchase. Briefs are characterized by fast, global electronic dissemination, standard publishing contracts, easy-to-use manuscript preparation and formatting guidelines, and expedited production schedules. We aim for publication 8-12 weeks after acceptance.

Francisco Simões • Emre Erdogan
Editors

NEETs in European rural areas

Individual features, support systems and policy measures

Editors
Francisco Simões
Cis-Iscte
Iscte
Lisbon, Portugal

Emre Erdogan
Department of International Relations
Istanbul Bilgi University
Eyüpsultan, Istanbul, Türkiye

ISSN 2212-6368　　　　　　　　ISSN 2212-6376　(electronic)
SpringerBriefs in Sociology
ISBN 978-3-031-45678-7　　　　ISBN 978-3-031-45679-4　(eBook)
https://doi.org/10.1007/978-3-031-45679-4

This work was supported by ISCTE – Instituto Universitário de Lisboa

© The Editor(s) (if applicable) and The Author(s) 2024. This book is an open access publication.
Open Access This book is licensed under the terms of the Creative Commons Attribution 4.0 International License (http://creativecommons.org/licenses/by/4.0/), which permits use, sharing, adaptation, distribution and reproduction in any medium or format, as long as you give appropriate credit to the original author(s) and the source, provide a link to the Creative Commons license and indicate if changes were made.
The images or other third party material in this book are included in the book's Creative Commons license, unless indicated otherwise in a credit line to the material. If material is not included in the book's Creative Commons license and your intended use is not permitted by statutory regulation or exceeds the permitted use, you will need to obtain permission directly from the copyright holder.
The use of general descriptive names, registered names, trademarks, service marks, etc. in this publication does not imply, even in the absence of a specific statement, that such names are exempt from the relevant protective laws and regulations and therefore free for general use.
The publisher, the authors, and the editors are safe to assume that the advice and information in this book are believed to be true and accurate at the date of publication. Neither the publisher nor the authors or the editors give a warranty, expressed or implied, with respect to the material contained herein or for any errors or omissions that may have been made. The publisher remains neutral with regard to jurisdictional claims in published maps and institutional affiliations.

This Springer imprint is published by the registered company Springer Nature Switzerland AG
The registered company address is: Gewerbestrasse 11, 6330 Cham, Switzerland

Paper in this product is recyclable.

Acknowledgment

This publication is based upon work from COST Action CA 18213: Rural NEET Youth Network: Modeling the risks underlying NEETs social exclusion, supported by COST (European Cooperation in Science and Technology).

COST (European Cooperation in Science and Technology) is a funding agency for research and innovation networks. Our Actions help connect research initiatives across Europe and enable scientists to grow their ideas by sharing them with their peers. This boosts their research, career and innovation.

www.cost.eu.

Introduction

We are living in the era of polycrisis "a set of interconnected challenges that are having a devastating impact on people and the planet (Henig & Knight, 2023)." The recent COVID-19 pandemic has resulted in widespread mortality, illness, and economic devastation. In addition it has exacerbated existing disparities and vulnerabilities. The conflict in Ukraine has caused a humanitarian crisis, as millions of people have been displaced from their homes. Moreover, the on-going war has disrupted the global food and energy markets, driving up prices and causing food insecurity and poverty. Extreme weather events, such as floods, droughts, and heat waves, are becoming more frequent due to climate change. These events are displacing people, damaging food production, and destroying livelihoods. In many countries, inequality is increasing, leaving a growing number of individuals behind. This inequality makes people more susceptible to crises and harder to recover from them. As a consequence, polarization is increasing worldwide as political, social, and economic divisions become more pronounced. This polarization makes finding common ground and addressing shared challenges more difficult (Dijsktra et al., 2020).

A context of polycrisis requires new responses from States, particularly for dealing with the so-called complex social problems, meaning those that do not conform to linear solutions and instead require collaboration between stakeholders for policies vertical and horizontal coordination (Klijn & Koppenjan, 2014). The situation of young people Not in Employment, nor in Education or Training (NEETs) corresponds perfectly to the definition of a complex social problem. However, to date, policies targeting NEETs are often focused on the economic dimension of the problem, framing it as a failure of the labor market. These policies are developed based on a top-down approach, departing from international and national authorities and usually neglecting the involvement of local actors and their target populations, namely young people. Gender, ethnicity, and having an immigrant background are intersecting factors that further complicate the definition of policies for NEETs. The recent Reinforced Youth Guarantee (YG) of the European Union provides an opportunity for developing "better" policies. This framework may come to promote tailored and individualized approaches to young people, considering differences between different NEET profiles. In addition to the development of bottom-up, coordinated policies, addressing NEETs requirements demands for a territorialized approach from the scientific community, one that clearly distinguishes urban from rural NEETs paying particular attention to the latter. This call for scientific action is needed considering that NEET rates across the European Union tend to be higher in rural areas, particularly in Southern and Eastern countries which are precisely the ones showing bigger inequalities between cities and the countryside (Simões et al., 2022).

This book is based on a collective effort made by the members of the COST Action 18213 Rural NEET Youth Network: Modeling the risks underlying rural NEETs social exclusion (https://rnyobservatory.eu/web/) to respond to the identified policy and knowledge gaps. Specifically, this book has two main aims. Firstly, we intend to share collective insights about the main features of rural NEETs and promising interventions aiming at this subgroup of NEETs. Secondly, we also expect to inspire the development of better policies targeting NEETs overall, but especially for those living in the countryside. The experience of the Rural NEET Youth Network of developing a common perspective covering a large geographical scope (30 countries) as well as the attention given to different profiles of NEETs was crucial to underline the importance of building up-to-date knowledge and more flexible policies.

The knowledge produced by the members of the Rural NEET Youth Network demands an ecological understanding of NEETs. Therefore we drew on Bronfenbrenner's (1979) bioecological model. This theoretical framework is rooted in developmental psychology and analyzes how the interactions between different systems in an individual's environment influence their development. The framework is comprised of five levels: microsystem, mesosystem, exosystem, macrosystem, and chronosystem. The microsystem consists of the individual's immediate environment, including family, school, and peers. The mesosystem comprises the interactions between several microsystems, such as the connection between a person's home and school. The exosystem consists of social settings that indirectly affect the individual, such as a parent's workplace. The macrosystem comprises the cultural and societal values and beliefs that shape the environment of the individual. The chronosystem covers the historical and temporal environment within which the growth of an individual occurs.

The bioecological model proposes that individual development can stem from various environmental levels, thus recognizing that both risks and opportunities for personal development require a holistic and dynamic view of several interactive elements. The interactive element of the bioecological model is described by the PPCT (Process, Person, Context, and Time) formula of the bioecological model. The Process element of the model addresses the specific mechanisms by which issues or dangers arise, such as cognitive or emotional processes. The Person factor evaluates individual traits, such as temperament or cognitive ability, that may make a person more or less sensitive to issues or hazards. The Context component takes into account the various systems in an individual's surroundings, such as family, school, and community, that may contribute to personal development and protect against risks. The Time dimension addresses the dynamic nature of growth, as well as how past and present settings may influence the emergence of problems or dangers (Bronfenbrenner, 1979).

Overall, the chapters that constitute this book address the bioecological understanding of rural NEETs in many different, but complementary ways.

The first chapter of our book is an overview of rural NEETs main individual features. In this respect, Francisco Simões starts by emphasizing the key role of educational attainment and gender in shaping rural NEETs trajectories. He specifically emphasizes that becoming and staying in the NEET category in the countryside is mainly driven by low qualifications and also by gender stereotypes affecting young women. These two factors end up shaping rural NEETs psychosocial profiles. Indeed, rural women in the NEET condition are more often inactive NEETs dedicated to family care duties, seem to develop a more negative understanding of professional choices and present worse well-being levels, especially when compared to urban female NEETs. In turn, rural men in the NEET condition are more often unemployed NEETs, combining over and again precariousness and unemployment spells in low-paid and low-skilled jobs, ending up accepting their professional circumstances as a kind of normality. This chapter lays, therefore, the ground for understanding how factors interacting at other levels of the bioecological model shape rural NEETs personal characteristics.

The second chapter of our book co-authored by Ferreira et al. expands Simões' approach by uncovering the factors that facilitate community-based projects for effectively supporting NEETs in rural areas with the aim of promoting their quality of life and social inclusion. To address their goal, the authors use empirical data collected by Working Group 1 from the Rural NEET Youth Network for five grassroots projects cutting across different European countries (Portugal, Italy, Lithuania, Sweden, and North Macedonia). Their line of inquiry is mostly situated at the mesosystem level of the bioecological model, although their work continuously questions the interactions between the relevant stakeholders operating at that level as well as at other levels of the bioecological model. Their findings demonstrate that the sustainability of community-based projects aiming at rural young people including those fitting the NEET condition depends on the local dimension in terms of departing from young people's needs and participation and duly addressing local communities' challenges. These projects' capacity to create and consolidate partnerships is identified as their main strength. In turn, rural young people's lack of motivation and negative representations about the countryside, as well as the limited support from local institutions (e.g., schools), are seen as the biggest threats to the sustained development of these local initiatives targeting rural young people.

The work by Flynn et al., in the third chapter of this book, extends some of the conclusions of the chapter authored by Ferreira et al. to the educational sector. The authors of this chapter focus on formal and non-formal education policies and interventions taking place in EU (Italy, Estonia, Latvia, and Portugal) and non-EU countries (Albania) to improve rural young people's prospect to reengage with learning environments and projects, to address the importance of formal education and skills development or to prevent early school leaving. Departing from the short description of case studies analyzed during the operation of the Working Group 2 of the Rural NEET Youth Network, the authors once again highlight that local sensitivity and contextualization are key characteristics of any successful education policy or program aiming at vulnerable young people, particularly in rural areas. They also suggest that this premise holds true throughout different levels of the bioecological model (from the macrosystem to the microsystem) and across different educational domains (vocational education and training, NEET outreach, or non-formal education projects).

In the fourth chapter, Petrescu et al. reflect on multiple inputs offered by Working Group 3 from the Rural NEET Youth Network, which focused on employment and employment services for rural NEETs. The authors specifically explore the main features of the Reinforced Youth Guarantee (RYG), before providing an in-depth analysis of its implementation across six European countries, to understand if the measures included in the national plans are tailored across different types of territories (rural and non-rural). This analysis is relevant and timely as the adoption of the RYG has been slow across EU member. Petrescu et al. demonstrate that Spain is the only country were there are specific measures dedicated to NEETs from rural, remote and disadvantaged areas. The authors also show that in Lithuania, Spain, Romania, Poland and Italy there have been issued some measures for specific categories of NEETs which may indirectly benefit some specific sub-groups of rural NEETs such as young women or long-term unemployed young people.

The fifth chapter of this book, authored by Mujčinović et al., offers a specific ecological approach to rural development issues. This chapter prepared by the Working Group 4 of the Rural NEET Youth Network aims at proposing a holistic model for upholding rural young people's entrepreneurship, with a particular focus on young farmers. Their approach combines the concepts of resilience, sustainability, and multifunctionality of rural areas, duly supported by current technological developments, to propose a framework that can help new, innovative businesses to flourish in the countryside, representing therefore an opportunity for young farmers to prosper, but also for vulnerable groups such as rural young women or rural NEETs to find jobs. The authors also pinpoint barriers to the implementation of their model, while acknowledging that existing policy frameworks (e.g., Green Deal) bring attached new possibilities to empower rural areas and take them to another level.

In the sixth and final chapter of this book, Erdogan and Paabort look into how new policy development models are needed to better address NEETs expectations and requirements, irrespective of their geolocation. This chapter is an outcome of Working Group 5 of the Rural NEET Youth Network as one of its priorities was to focus on policies aiming at NEETs. The authors start by describing the limitations of the classic, rationalistic approach to NEETs, which is excessively focused on efficiency and economic-led outcomes. They further substantiate their position based on a survey conducted with the Rural NEET Youth Network members. As an alternative, they propose that policy development for NEETs must be anchored on design-thinking and co-creation approaches that duly lead to the stakeholders' involvement, human-centered policy measures and value creation for the whole society. For this matter, they present the process upholding the new Estonian YG

Plan as a case from which other countries can draw conclusions to update their policy development approach aiming at NEETs.

Overall, this book is an original scientific contribution to address rural NEETs, while always taking into account how this knowledge can contribute to new policy measures which are more attuned to vulnerable rural young people's needs. Indeed, at the end of each chapter, the reader will find a systematized list of suggestions for new research developments as well as policy recommendations. This means, therefore, that at all times the authors were committed to the Rural NEET Youth Network's vision of developing interdisciplinary, internationally based knowledge to inform policymaking at regional, national, and international levels.

Iscte – Instituto Universitário de Lisboa,   Francisco Simões
Lisbon, Portugal
Department of International Relations,   Emre Erdogan
Istanbul Bilgi University, Istanbul,
Turkey

References

Bronfenbrenner, U. (1979). *The ecology of human development: Experiments by nature and design*. Harvard University Press.

Dijsktra, L., Poelman, H., & Rodríguez-Pose, A. (2020). The geography of EU discontent. *Regional Studies, 54*(6), 737–753. https://doi.org/10.1080/00343404.2019.1654603

Henig, D., & Knight, D. M. (2023). Polycrisis: Prompts for an emerging worldview. *Antropology Today, 39*(2), 3–6. https://doi.org/10.1111/1467-8322.12793

Klijn E.H., & Koppenjan, J. (2014). Complexity in governance network theory. *Complexity Governance & Networks, 1*(1), 61–70. https://doi.org/10.7564/14-CGN8

Simões, F., Erdogan, E., Muratovic, M., & Syk, D. (2022). Scrutinising the exceptionalism of young rural NEETs: A bibiliometric review. *Youth & Society, 54* (2S), 8S–28S. https://doi.org/10.7711/07074/0401414181X82X1210104400534

Contents

1 **Rural NEETs: Individual Features, Challenges, and Opportunities**.................................... 1
Francisco Simões

2 **Building Bridges: Community-Based Projects for Participation and Social Inclusion of Rural NEETs**........................ 17
Tatiana Ferreira, Adriano Mauro Ellena, Frida Jonsson, Belém Barbosa, Pınar Uyan-Semerci, Emelj Tuna, Giedrė Kvieskienė, Elena Marta, İlkay Unay-Gailhard, and Maria Fernandes-Jesus

3 **Rural NEETs: Pathways Through Formal and Non-formal Education**... 35
Paul Flynn, Heidi Paabort, Valentina Milenkova, Katerina Bojkovska, Antonella Rocca, Liena Hačatrjana, Vladislava Lendzhova, Albena Nakova, and Marta de Oliveira Rodrigues

4 **Rural Dimension of the Employment Policies for NEETs. A Comparative Analysis of the Reinforced Youth Guarantee**....... 51
Claudia Petrescu, Ruta Braziene, Òscar Prieto-Flores, Mariano Soler, Anastasia Costantini, Bianca Buligescu, Daiva Skuciene, Antonella Rocca, Federica Pizzolante, Luca Koltai, Mateusz Smoter, and Sylwia Danilowska

5 **Pathways for Young Farmers' Entrepreneurship in Sustainable Rural Development**................................... 69
Alen Mujčinović, Štefan Bojnec, Aleksandra Nikolić, Anita Bušljeta Tonković, Slaven Gašparović, Messaoud Lazereg, Anđelka Stojanović, and Daniela Bojadjieva

6 **A More Youth-Centered Policy Development Perspective in NEET Policies**....................................... 89
Emre Erdoğan and Heidi Paabort

Chapter 1
Rural NEETs: Individual Features, Challenges, and Opportunities

Francisco Simões

Abstract In this chapter, I present and discuss the main individual features of rural young people Not in Employment, nor in Education and Training (NEET) living in rural areas. These characteristics fit in the so-called individual system of the bioecological model. I start out by depicting rural NEETs educational background and gender differences within this subset of NEETs, due to their importance in shaping these young people's pathways. Afterward, I elaborate on what is known to date about rural NEETs psychological profile, particularly regarding their cognitive skills, soft skills, and well-being. Finally, I will explore how these personal characteristics of rural NEETs may interact with emerging challenges and opportunities in rural communities located at other layers of the bioecological model. This chapter strongly relies on several contributions from the COST Action Rural NEET Youth Network, as well as on the most relevant international scholarship and policy reports focusing on rural communities' development, youth employment, and school-to-work transition, to achieve an interdisciplinary understanding of rural NEETs individual traits and features.

Keywords NEETs · Rurality · Educational background · Gender · Cognitive skills · Well-being

1.1 Introduction

Young people Not in Employment, nor in Education or Training (NEET) constitute a controversial social category. Since the seminal work by Furlong (2006), the NEET definition has been targeted for being mostly a statistical tool combining young people with very different educational, social, or economic backgrounds under the same label. Meanwhile, the concern with this group diversity has spread across research efforts dedicated to identifying distinct subgroups of NEETs or the multiple

---

F. Simões (✉)
Iscte – Instituto Universitário de Lisboa, Lisbon, Portugal
e-mail: Francisco.Simoes@iscte-iul.pt

© The Author(s) 2024
F. Simões, E. Erdogan (eds.), *NEETs in European rural areas*, SpringerBriefs in Sociology, https://doi.org/10.1007/978-3-031-45679-4_1

pathways that these young people trail in the transition from school to work. More recently, drawing on previous efforts brought forward by the Eurofound (2012), Mascherini (2019) has developed a NEETs typology departing from these young people's work status. Specifically, Mascherini proposes that one can distinguish between re-entrants, short-term and long-term unemployed NEETs, inactive NEETs due to multiple reasons such as family care, and physical or mental health issues, and voluntary NEETs who are in this condition based on personal options such as traveling or taking a sabbatical year.

Despite the justified concerns with its homogenization drive, it is important to acknowledge that the NEET notion has helped to demonstrate the tremendous social and economic losses associated with being in this condition. Indeed, states, communities, families, and, above all, young people are faced with an overwhelming social and economic burden of becoming and remaining in the NEET status (Eurofound, 2012). Consequently, for the past decade, European Union countries have coordinated their policy response to systematically address high shares of NEETs, especially in the aftermath of the 2008 economic crisis, under the Youth Guarantee framework (Tosun et al., 2019). Alongside, several empirical and policy reports established the ever-increasing risks associated with the NEET condition, as the shift from the role of student to the role of worker became longer (Pastore et al., 2021), more uncertain (Schoon, 2020) and detached from institutional support (Cuzzocrea, 2020).

A more nuanced understanding of these young people's experiences and developmental paths, one that duly informs policies and interventions and goes beyond their educational or work status, is still pretty much missing. One important add-on to a more refined research agenda in this field consists in examining the intersection between the NEET status with spatialities. Overall, younger generations living in urban, suburban, and rural areas navigate along disparate socioeconomic challenges and opportunities. There is mounting evidence, however, showing that territorial disparities at the subnational level are growing, with strong and more negative implications for school-to-work transition (Schoon, 2020), youth employment (Cefalo & Scandurra, 2021), and NEETs living in less affluent areas (Simões et al., 2022). Furthermore, the official statistics confirm the need to combine geolocation with the NEET status to improve the on-the-ground policy response. While there was a significant decrease in rural NEETs shares for the past decade across the European continent, rural NEET shares remained as one dimension of the structural divide between more and less affluent areas, but also a key element of the North/South or East/West asymmetries affecting the European Union (Simões, 2022). According to Fig. 1.1, in 2020, NEET rates were higher in rural areas (18.80%) compared with suburban (14.40%) and urban areas (16.00%). This trend was evident in 13 out of 27 EU countries. More importantly, however, this difference was remarkable in Southern (e.g., Greece) and Eastern European countries (e.g., Hungary and Romania)—by 10, 15, or even 20 percentual points (Eurostat, 2021).

Bearing in mind both the academic discussions as well as the statistical trends, in this chapter I focus on describing the individual features of rural NEETs. My effort fits into the most concentric level of the bioecological model, the theoretical

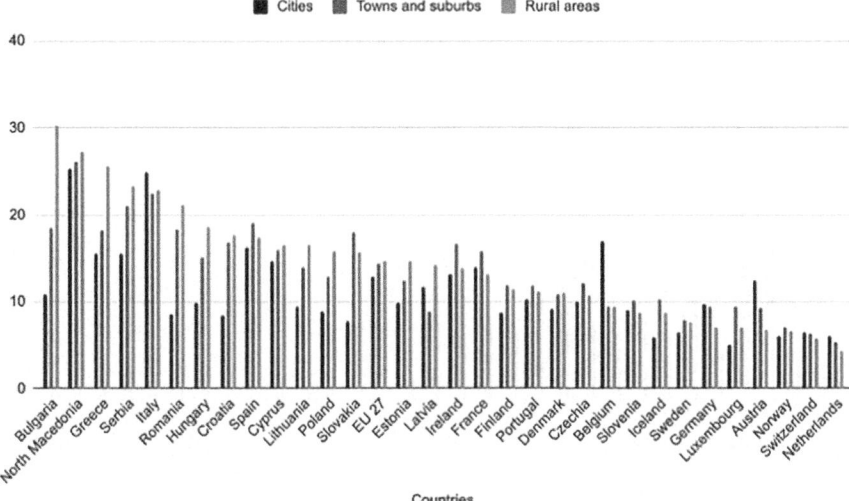

Fig. 1.1 NEET share by the degree of urbanization in European countries (%). Source: Eurostat—Labour Force Survey [EDAT_LFSE_29]; data extraction on 27.01.23; Notes: Countries excluded had no data for rural areas (e.g., Malta); the estimates for 2021 were still not definitive for most of the countries

framework inspiring the Rural NEET Youth Network mission to develop a more systematic understanding of this group of young people. According to the bioecological model, the individual level encompasses the organic-hereditary traits as well as psychological traits, including skills and behaviors (Bronfenbrenner & Morris, 2006). Following this theoretical stance, I will depict rural NEETs core features in terms of educational background and gender differences, before elaborating on what is known to date about their psychological profile. Finally, I will discuss how these personal characteristics of rural NEETs may interact with emerging challenges and opportunities in rural communities. To fulfill my aim, I will strongly rely on several contributions from the Rural NEET Youth Network, as well as on the most relevant international scholarship and policy reports focusing on rural communities' development, youth employment, and school-to-work transition, in order to achieve an interdisciplinary understanding of rural NEETs.

1.2 Who Are Rural NEETs?

1.2.1 Low Educational Status: A Key Risk for Becoming a Rural NEET

International research efforts have long established that students in remote, less affluent, and mostly rural areas struggle to excel in education. There are, indeed, a

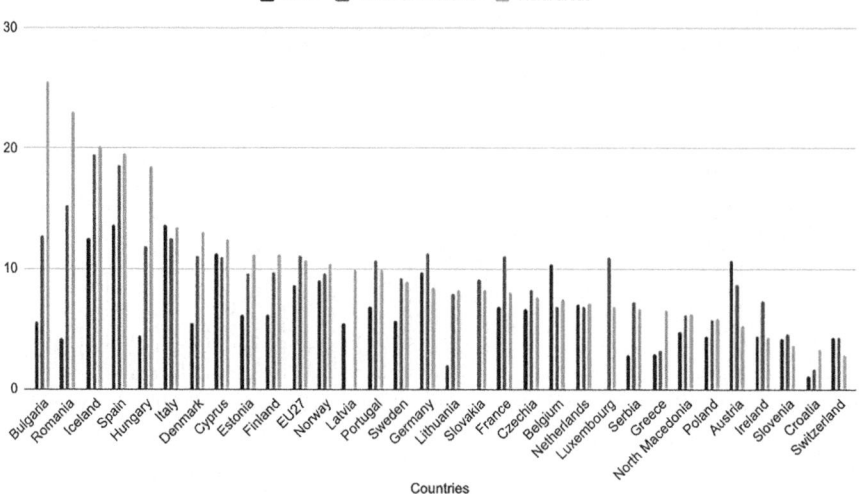

Fig. 1.2 Early School Leaving from Education and Training by the degree of urbanization across European Countries and the EU, in 2020 (%). Source: Eurostat—Labour Force Survey [EDAT_LFSE_30]; data extraction on 24.01.23; Notes: Countries excluded had no data for rural areas (e.g., Malta) or for all levels of urbanization (e.g., Latvia); the data available for 2021 was still not definitive for most of the countries

few reports (e.g., Bæck, 2016) showing that rural students' results are usually outperformed by the results of their counterparts attending schools located in suburban and urban areas.

For instance, in secondary education, rural students' poorer performance often translates into higher dropout rates (Bæck, 2016). The same applies to other indicators. Figure 1.2 summarizes the Early School Leaving from Education and Training rates by the degree of urbanization, in 2020, across several European countries. The graphic display shows how this pivotal indicator of the school-to-work transition is worse, overall, in the EU27 rural areas. This trend was evident in 21 out of the 30 countries included in the analysis. Several social and structural reasons have been put forward to explain these territorial disparities in educational outcomes.

At the social level, rural areas present larger socioeconomic inequalities, meaning that a more significant part of the population is in greater material, social and cultural privation (Bæck, 2016). Therefore, students originating in more vulnerable rural households have more limited access to symbolic, cultural, or technological artifacts, such as books or computers (Simões et al., 2022). Moreover, the educational expectations of socioeconomically disadvantaged rural parents regarding their children, as well as their involvement in school are lower, especially when compared to the smaller proportion of rural parents who have privileged access to resources (Bæck, 2016). Such inequalities are further stretched by a frequent mismatch between school values and rural communities' worldviews. Schools position the future of young generations in affluent territories, such as cities, contrary to the prevalent traditional norms and values of rural communities (Simões et al., 2021).

The risk of rural students' educational underperformance affecting NEETs is further extended by structural factors, beginning with the on-the-ground infrastructure. Schools in low-density territories, such as rural areas, mountain regions, or border regions are often far from students' homes or at perennial risk of being shut down (Bæck, 2016). Rural students' learning and school attainment are also limited by greater resource shortages (Sullivan et al., 2013), although this caveat also treathens, for instance, schools in suburban areas (Silva & Abrantes, 2017). Moreover, the quality and retention of teachers in rural areas are lower with a strong potential to negatively affect school results (Reagan et al., 2019). Having a permanent contract means teachers face fewer mobility problems and can be more committed to their students in the long run. Lower teacher retention rates are further complicated by greater challenges inherent to the school-parent relationship, due to these communities' close social ties and bigger potential for clashes between parents' and schools' worldviews (Bæck, 2016).

There is, however, a consensus forming that rural students' educational results would benefit from a more granular analysis and stronger causal interpretation (e.g., Bæck, 2016). Missing a more systematic examination of rural education outcomes may lead to an unnecessary and deceiving fatalistic narrative about rural education. For instance, while urban/rural gaps in early school leaving from education and training rates are quite big in some Eastern and Southern countries such as Bulgaria, Romania, or Spain, these disparities are much smaller in several countries across the continent. Concurrently, territorial disparities in education by the degree of urbanization are becoming less straightforward. For instance, some urban and suburban areas, such as the suburban belts of major cities, do display growingly worrisome educational outcomes. As Silva and Abrantes (2017) point out, many high-density, suburban areas have become more diverse from a cultural point of view, but also more socially vulnerable. These communities often rely on public services and programs instead of extended families for accessing services such as education, but also to find social and instrumental support. Subsequently, educational programs struggle to respond to students' growing diverse backgrounds, with negative impacts on school outcomes. In sum, a true spatialized approach to the educational risks of becoming and remaining NEETs must consider the dynamic changes in local, subnational, and cross-national trends that come to affect school population composition and the subsequent allocation of resources.

1.2.2 Gender and Educational Status: A Decisive Intersection for Rural NEETs

Educational attainment has distinct implications for rural young men and women. Specifically, the intersection between education performance and gender influences the odds of becoming a rural NEET through processes such as spatial mobilities or education and professional expectations.

Prior reports have shown that women are overrepresented in rural youth out-migration fluxes (Farrugia, 2016; Leibert, 2016). Compared to rural young men, rural young women show greater educational aspirations and display higher professional expectations that drive them to move to more affluent suburban and urban areas, seeking a university degree as well as more qualified and well-paid jobs. Consequently, rural female NEETs are mostly the less educated women who opt to stay or who do not have enough financial resources to leave. These women are more likely to be dedicated to family care duties and, consequently, face a greater risk of remaining for larger periods in a NEET condition (Mascherini, 2019; Sadler et al., 2015). Moreover, the rural labour markets offer chiefly male-dominated jobs in agriculture or small industries (Leibert, 2016). Traditional gender stereotypes which are more prevalent in rural areas limit even further women's professional fulfillment outside the household (Farrugia, 2016). Rural women face, thus, a greater danger of being inactive NEETs, meaning that they are among those struggling the most to return to the job market (Mascherini, 2019).

The gloomy prospects for rural female NEETs do not mean that rural young men are outshining in the school-to-work transition. To begin with, young men are staying or establishing themselves in many European rural areas in disproportionately higher numbers (Leibert, 2016). This puts them competing for mostly low-qualified, temporary, and very precarious jobs in a narrow rural economy dominated by sectors such as agriculture (Almeida & Simões, 2020). They have, therefore, a higher chance of being in and out, but also for longer periods in the NEET category as short-term or long-term unemployed (Mascherini, 2019). Despite the mounting disadvantage resulting from these vulnerable professional trajectories, young men tend to adjust to this situation. Low-paid, precarious jobs are accepted as a fatality, and being aware of the local labor market conditions may even make them feel more competent (Almeida & Simões, 2020).

1.2.3 *Rural NEETs Self-Perceptions: Cognitive Skills, Soft Skills, and Well-Being*

In recent years, there is a body of literature that has started to examine the psychological features of NEETs such as their mental health (Simões et al., 2022). Nevertheless, the psychological profiling of rural NEETs is limited to only a few papers coming out from research projects conducted in Portugal (Simões et al., 2017; Almeida & Simões, 2020) and Italy (Ellena et al., 2021). As Schoon (2020) rightly states, the understanding of the school-to-work transition is, nevertheless, incomplete if the role of psychological factors is not added to the influence of social and structural factors shaping this vital dimension of becoming an adult.

One domain in which the psychological functioning of emergent adults is key for tailoring school-to-work transition is the modeling of vocational and professional choices. Two main mechanisms guide these choices. The first one, circumscription, corresponds to a definition of vocational preferences across childhood and adolescence, resulting in a delimitation of acceptable future professional alternatives. The second one, compromise, consists of personal investment in some areas seen as more realistic and accessible in the transition to adulthood. This individual adjustment results in dropping-out occupational preferences considered aspirational or idealistic, in a process fuelled by multiple individual (e.g., gender stereotypes) or contextual (e.g., economic hardship) factors (Gottfredson, 2002).

The circumscription and compromise mechanisms mobilize a comprehensive set of cognitive skills to clarify vocational and professional choices. Among them are metacognitive and planning skills such as self-efficacy, defined as personal beliefs that one can be successful by generating the desired outcomes for a determined task (Bandura, 1997), outcome expectations, referring to judgments limited to the most likely or realistic consequences of a certain behavior (Beal & Crockett, 2010), as well as perceived barriers, composed of current or future constraints to vocational development identified by individuals, as opposed to objective barriers such as educational level or income (Lent et al., 2000). Alongside metacognitive and planning skills, future-time cognitions also play an important role in shaping vocational decisions, with hope being one of them. Hope is a bi-dimensional psychological attribute encompassing the perceived capacity to achieve goals also known as pathways and a successful sense of goal-directed energy labeled as agency (Snyder, 2000). Overall, vulnerable emergent adults such as NEETs show lower educational qualifications, face more recurrent and longer unemployment spells, lack access to quality education, vocational guidance, and consistent professional experiences, denote a lower self-efficacy (Mortimer et al., 2016), perceive more barriers to find a job or to secure a contract (Messersmith & Schulenberg, 2008), and downgrade their professional expectations, as they anticipate to find less-qualified, lower paid jobs (Diemer et al., 2010).

A few studies have tried to untangle the factors associated with rural NEETs metacognitive and strategic planning skills (Simões et al., 2017; Almeida & Simões, 2020). These reports demonstrate how employment-related factors are key in shaping this group's psychological features. Greater stability in terms of having secured at least one job contract strengthens self-efficacy perceptions, contrary to longer unemployment spells (>24 months). Interestingly, though, greater self-efficacy among rural NEETs is also associated with lower independence levels, measured by living in the parental household. While this result is counterintuitive (more independence is usually associated with stronger self-efficacy beliefs), living in the parental household seems to be a proxy measure for mutual social support. Parental support, whether emotional, instrumental, or both, can help children feel more confident in their own abilities during the transition to adulthood. In parallel, these children in a NEET condition, such as females involved in caregiving tasks or males frequently engaged in unreported work, including small family businesses may more easily enact their own skills in the family context, thus demonstrating to themselves their personal abilities. Family can, thus, constitute the most immediate if not the only social context in which rural NEETs can demonstrate their skills (Simões et al., 2017), an interpretation that is aligned with the reported high levels of mutual informal support in rural areas (Simões et al., 2022).

According to the existent reports, rural NEETs cognitive skills involved in vocational choices also entail lower professional and educational expectations. Specifically, rural NEETs who have completed lower-level secondary education are more skeptical about attaining higher levels of qualification and finding more complex and higher-paid jobs. Interestingly, however, those who attain secondary education see room for improving their qualifications, which may be informative for policymaking (Simões et al., 2017). These predominantly pessimistic expectations contrast with the generalized irrelevance of demographic—(e.g., gender) or employment-related (e.g., time of unemployment) factors in predicting rural NEETs perceived professional barriers (Simões et al., 2017). Subsequent research efforts confirm, however, that women perceive fewer barriers to entering the job market. More importantly, these perceptions are fine-tuned when demographic factors are combined with other metacognitive and planning skills. For instance, higher levels of self-efficacy among male rural NEETs are associated with stronger anticipation of barriers, while men depicting weaker self-efficacy also show weaker perceived barriers, compared with women in identical conditions (Almeida & Simões, 2020). This intersection between gender, self-efficacy, and perceived barriers levels reflects, to some extent, the stronger involvement in the rural job market of male NEETs. As they are repeatedly exposed to risks such as unemployment, precariousness, or low-paid jobs, these men also feel more competent to navigate this hardship (Almeida & Simões, 2020). Thus, adversity among male NEETs in rural areas tends to be incorporated into their cognitive apparatus, with these views about the labor market being further strengthened by strict vocational gender stereotypes that more often limit men to uncertain, low-qualified, and physically demanding jobs in these territories (Bæck, 2016).

The understanding of future-oriented cognitions in rural NEETs professional development is less detailed in the literature. To my knowledge, only one report focuses on understanding the factors influencing rural NEETs hope levels (Simões, submitted). This study adopts a bioecological lens to assess how hope levels evolved among rural NEETs for 12 months during the COVID-19 pandemic. One main finding stemming from this investigation is that only one factor at the individual system level—gender—is directly associated with hope levels. Specifically, female rural NEETs present a significantly worse evolution on both hope dimensions (pathways and agency) compared to men, after accounting for factors at the macrosystem (e.g., collectivism perceptions), the exosystem (e.g., public employment support) or the microsystem (e.g., informal social support) of the bioecological model. The same report delivers important insights regarding how the combination of work status (inactive *vs.* unemployed) with formal support provided by public employment services relates to agency levels. Indeed, while inactive NEETs' agency estimates increase due to an increment in public employment services' support, unemployed NEETs' estimates decrease over time to a point that they are below inactive NEETs' agency rates at higher levels of public employment support. It is reasonable to assume that a larger digital coverage of these services during the COVID-19 pandemic improved outreaching inactive rural NEETs and nurturing their goal-seeking energy, particularly among female or disabled NEETs who are less likely to attend face-to-face meetings. In turn, during this period unemployed NEETs were struggling with the recent job loss, lockdowns, and the economic activity downturn. In other words, the perceived increasing support provided by public employment services was insufficient to promote goal-seeking energy among unemployed NEETs considering the complex economic environment (Eurofound, 2021).

Finally, at least one report has delved into the factors associated with the psychological well-being and soft skills of rural NEETs (Ellena et al., 2021). The first finding offered by this research piece was showing lower psychological well-being levels among women with lower qualifications, irrespectively of living in rural or urban areas. Female rural NEETs reported, however, worst psychological well-being compared to their urban counterparts. The accumulation of risks previously mentioned such as the high share of family caregivers that usually compose this group in rural areas (Sadler et al., 2015), the limited participation in the job market (Simões & Rio, 2020), but also the greater levels of social comparison in less affluent areas, leading to increased perceptions of failure (Ellena et al., 2021) jointly explain these outcomes. Similar results were found regarding soft skills self-assessment, with only one exception. Rural female NEETs with tertiary education living in rural areas presented a more positive vision of their skills, compared to female urban NEETs with an identical educational level. Although employment opportunities are scarcer in the countryside, these rural women may reason that their educational background is more unusual and therefore, more promising for securing a new job. They may also interpret that inactivity or unemployment are more transitory in rural areas than in cities, where job vacancies are more easily available, but intense professional competition can also raise more uncertainty when one assesses personal qualifications (Ellena et al., 2021).

1.3 Challenges Shaping the Individual Characteristics of Rural NEETs

What we know about rural NEETs individual characteristics is quite limited. Moreover, the available knowledge is expected to change in the years to come. New demographic, social, and economic trends are forming in rural spaces, proposing new challenges for younger generations, especially for the most vulnerable ones.

Rural NEETs are and will continue to be threatened by their invisibility. This specific group of NEETs is hard to be targeted by services and to be enrolled in on-the-ground active labor market policies (European Commission, 2018). This has implications for service deliverance in the employment and education domains.

In the employment domain, invisibility translates into limited capacity from public employment services to outreach to rural NEETs. According to Smoter (2022), outreach can be improved if public training and employment services are more effective in coordinating their actions with Non-Governmental Organizations (NGO) specialized in social and youth work. There is also the expectation that the growing digitalization of these services, particularly of public employment services, will expand the capacity of reaching out to NEETs in remote areas (European Commission, 2018). However, it is questionable that the digitization of services *per se* will effectively increase rural NEETs engagement with public officers. True digital transformation entails a full modification of organizational norms, values, and processes. Pilling up digital solutions on existing ill-analog processes will not result in better public digital encounters (Lindgren et al., 2019), nor it will immediately provide person-centered approaches tailored to young people facing very uncertain transitions from school to work. Therefore, the end goal of public employment services' digital transformation here is to find the right mix between analog support (e.g., street work, mentoring) and digital support, tailored to the characteristics of rural NEETs (Simões & Marta, 2024, in press). In any case, the serious challenges in targeting and engaging with rural NEETs constitute an important reminder that our knowledge of this group remains superficial.

Rural NEETs invisibility involves limited outreach, but also barriers to participation. This second layer of rural NEETs invisibility is particularly relevant in the education sector and can be defined as a generalized disregard for students' expectations, needs, and dreams when defining curricula or training programs, particularly for the most disadvantaged ones and who are, thus, at greater risk of becoming NEETs. As I have pointed out earlier, low education attainment represents a key risk shaping school-to-work transition in rural areas. While educational figures (e.g., early school leaving from education and training) are improving across European countries and regions, that improvement is slower in remote and predominantly rural areas (Simões, 2022). More importantly, it is uncertain, to say the least, that the education sector will succeed in better equipping young people in rural areas with the skills required by local job markets. Besides the limited on-the-ground physical infrastructure and the lower rates of teacher retention (Reagan et al., 2019), the curricula being offered in rural areas are limited, especially in the vocational education and training sector (Bettencourt et al., 2023). This results in failure from local educational authorities to address the existing demand for intermediate professionals (Bettencourt et al., 2023) as well as to match local economic opportunities with young people's employment needs (Simões & Rio, 2020).

Another foreseen challenge with impacts for rural NEET profiling is related to the side effects of a declining rural economy. The rural economy is overwhelmed by the dismantling of industrial capacity, and the consequent loss of trained and/or skilled human capital. This scenario leaves behind entire generations without the opportunity to learn and to be mentored by older professionals (Zipin et al., 2015). Moreover, agriculture remains a pivotal economic sector in the countryside, but not without problems. The sector is mostly an aging one, struggling to attract, and retain those outside the sector, including NEETs (Simões, 2018). There are exceptions to this negative scenario, with some regions showing a vigorous services sector able to offer a considerable number of jobs, including for young women (Corbett, 2007). Others are managing to modernize agricultural activities through eco-agriculture and thereby increase their value (Simões & Rio, 2020). However, the path to a job in rural areas remains narrower and that must be accounted for when interpreting rural NEETs rates.

1.4 Opportunities Shaping the Future of Rural NEETs

There are also opportunities on the horizon for the most vulnerable rural young people. Altogether, these opportunities may contribute to a more diversified and qualified labor market, attracting local and non-local young people. One of these opportunities is associated with the changing nature of youth mobilities in rural territories. Out migration to urban areas will, certainly, continue to prevail, anchored on narratives of human potential that resume personal success in achieving high educational and professional standards (Farrugia, 2016; Simões et al., 2021). However, these onward movements of rural younger generations will more often overlap with circular or returning mobilities. This shift is mostly driven by other factors at the individual level, such as a sense of belongingness to a community or feeling attached to local culture and traditions, or greater appreciation for rural areas' quality of life, in terms of being in contact with nature or showing a preference for a more sustainable lifestyle (Silva et al., 2021; Simões et al., 2021). The figures do show that something is already changing in the demographic composition of rural younger generations (Simões et al., 2022). For the past decade, the share of European young people living in rural areas has marginally declined from 27.40% in 2011 to 26.34% in 2020. However, in some countries, such as Denmark (+18.74 pp), France (+129.48 pp), Italy (+73.80 pp), or Germany (29.20 pp), the share of rural young people has been swiftly increasing. However, in countries such as Estonia (−52.08 pp) and Poland (−35.22 pp), or in Southern countries, such as Greece (−50.37 pp) or Spain (−52.30 pp) we can observe the opposite trend (Eurostat, 2022).

The developments, driving forces, and implications of the new rural demographic trends changing the structure of the rural youth population require more attention from researchers and policymakers. However, they may already be reflecting with the transformative processes associated with the twin (digital and green) transition. The digital transition can respond to some of the listed challenges faced by rural young people. Upcoming digital solutions may, for instance, help to expand the coverage of welfare, education, and employment services, especially by improving reaching out strategies aimed at those that are harder to target by public services. This may represent a true means for engaging young people in relevant programs and interventions if these strategies are combined with the right kind of analog support, as I have already stressed (European Commission, 2018). The pace of dematerializing services can also be increased, raising the number of young people working remotely from the countryside in demanding, sophisticated, and well-paid jobs (International Labor Organization, 2022). Still, accomplishing these opportunities must account for the need to improve young people's digital literacy, internet connectivity, and access to the most up-to-date equipment in rural areas (European Commission, 2018).

Alongside, the green transition will allow for an upgrade of farming activities, through innovation and greater use of digital tools. Moreover, farming is being increasingly combined with services to increase its economic value (e.g., ecotourism). At the same time, sustainability needs are increasingly emphasizing the importance of closer supply chains and local consumerism (Unay-Gaillhard & Simões, 2021). Taken together, these changes can lead to a more diversified vocational education and training sector reflecting local opportunities and upholding more rewarding and decent jobs, as the green transition principles rely on all sustainability pillars (natural, social, and economic). Nevertheless, threats associated with intensive farming still expanding in many European countries must not be overseen, especially those that bring in young migrants, often through human trafficking networks, without any concern whatsoever for the welfare of these people or their social integration in local communities.

1.5 Conclusion

This chapter focused on describing the individual characteristics of rural NEETs. My effort focused, therefore, on detailing the features of the rural NEET individual system, the most concentric level of the bioecological model (Bronfenbrenner & Morris, 2006). I embarked on an exploration covering empirical and policy reports, always considering how factors operating at more external layers of the bioecological model (e.g., social support, official services) may shape individual characteristics of this vulnerable group.

The picture composed in the previous sections shows that rural NEETs constitute mostly an under-educated group, more often observed in Southern and Eastern European countries, who opt to stay in or lack the means to leave their communities in search for better opportunities. However, the experience of becoming and/or remaining in the NEET condition is quite different for women and men. Women are more often inactive NEETs dedicated to family care duties, seem to develop a more negative view of professional choices, and present worse well-being levels, especially when compared to urban female NEETs. Men are more often unemployed NEETs, combining over and again precariousness and unemployment spells in low-paid and low-skilled jobs, ending up accepting their professional circumstances as being normal.

1.5.1 New Research Developments

The body of research dedicated to rural NEETs psychological profiling is still limited in thematic and geographic scope. A whole research agenda on this area is needed, covering the following topics.

- **Comparing the individual and psychological features of rural and non-rural NEETs.** With only one exception (Ellena et al., 2021), the reports on rural NEETs do not follow a comparative effort to understand the specific features of NEETs living in different types of territories. This closer looker is required to better inform territorialized policies and interventions.
- **Diversifying the scope of psychological attributes included in new research efforts.** The analysis of psychological features of rural NEETs has focused mostly on their metacognitive skills. Knowing more about these psychological features is key to inform interventions aiming at improving school-to-work transition in rural areas. However, it is vital that psychological profiling of rural NEETs also covers mental health, well-being, or quality of life outcomes, considering this group's invisibility as well as the more limited access to social, economic, or cultural resources in the countryside.
- **Considering the intersection between gender and psychological features.** Although evidence is still scarce, it seems certain that female and male rural NEETs have very distinct educational and employment experiences. They also seem to interpret these experiences in disparate ways. Forthcoming research projects must systematically examine how women and men reason about these experiences, as both groups face specific risks that need to be addressed.

1.5.2 Policy Recommendations

Recommendations for policy development must be cautiously drafted considering the limited existing evidence about the individual profile of rural NEETs. Still, two lines of action seem relevant.

- **Improving outreach is urgent. Many rural NEETs remain invisible.** The combination of appropriate human-mediated or analogue support with digital tools may constitute a step forward. Investing in more mobile services, especially in more remote areas seems another step needed. Also improving the participation of young people in tailoring education and employment services is duly required. The absence of rural NEETs voices in the definition of programs and services constitutes a layer of their invisibility that seriously needs to be tackled.
- **On-the-ground programs must be gender sensitive.** The existing reports show that gender-blind interventions for rural NEETs will certainly constitute a waste of time and resources. Women will for sure benefit from measures such as more public-funded kindergartens vacancies or digital support from public

employment agencies, in case they want to find a job. Men, instead, are more likely to need support to improve their skills and qualifications to have access to more stable jobs. In any case, interventions must seek to fulfil person-centered approaches, always considering the striking individual differences between rural female and male NEETs.

References

Almeida, A., & Simões, F. (2020). Professional development perspectives across gender and age groups of under-qualified rural NEETs. *Journal of Community Psychology, 48*(5), 1620–1636. https://doi.org/10.1002/jcop.22356

Bæck, U. D. K. (2016). Rural location and academic success – remarks on research, contextualisation and methodology. *Scandinavian Journal of Educational Research, 60*(4), 435–448. https://doi.org/10.1080/00313831.2015.102416

Bandura, A. (1997). *Self-efficacy*. W. H. Freeman.

Beal, S. J., & Crockett, L. J. (2010). Adolescents' occupational and educational aspirations and expectations: Links to high school activities and adult educational attainment. *Developmental Psychology, 46*(1), 258–265. https://doi.org/10.1037/a0017416

Bettencourt, L., Simões, F., & Fernandes, B. (2023). Designing vocational training policies in an outermost European region: Highlights from a participatory process. *European Educational Research Journal*, 1–20. (in press). https://doi.org/10.1177/14749041231157445

Bronfenbrenner, U., & Morris, P. A. (2006). The bioecological model of human development. In R. M. Lerner & W. Damon (Eds.), *Handbook of child psychology: Theoretical models of human development* (pp. 793–828). Wiley.

Cefalo, R., & Scandurra, R. (2021). Territorial disparities in youth about market chances in Europe. *Regional Studies, Regional Science., 8*(1), 228–238. https://doi.org/10.1080/21681376.2021.1925580

Corbett, M. (2007). All kinds of potential: Women and out-migration in an Atlantic Canadian coastal community. *Journal of Rural Studies, 23*(4), 430–442. https://doi.org/10.1016/j.jrurstud.2006.12.001

Cuzzocrea, V. (2020). A place for mobility in metaphors of youth transitions. *Journal of Youth Studies, 23*(1), 61–75. https://doi.org/10.1080/13676261.2019.1703918

Diemer, M. A., Wang, Q., Moore, T., Gregory, S. R., Hatcher, K. M., & Voight, A. M. (2010). Sociopolitical development, work salience, and vocational expectations among low socioeconomic status African American, Latin American, and Asian American Youth. *Developmental Psychology, 46*(3), 619–635. https://doi.org/10.1037/a0017049

Ellena, M. A., Marta, E., Simões, F., Fernandes-Jesus, M., & Petrescu, C. (2021). Soft skills and psychological well-being: A Study on Italian rural and urban NEETs. *Calitatea Vieții, 32*(4), 1–19. https://doi.org/10.46841/RCV.2021.04.02

Eurofound. (2012). *NEETs-young people not in employment, education or training: Characteristics, costs and policy responses in Europe*. Publications Office of the European Union. https://op.europa.eu/en/publication-detail/-/publication/b657042d-ea99-11e5-a2a7-01aa75ed71a1

Eurofound. (2021). *Impact of COVID-19 on young people in the EU*. Publications Office of the European Union. Accessed August 25, 2022, from https://www.eurofound.europa.eu/sites/default/files/ef_publication/field_ef_document/ef20036en.pdf

European Commission. (2018). *Effective outreach to NEETs: Experience from the ground*. https://op.europa.eu/en/publication-detail/-/publication/ce7e7e0d-c5ec-11e8-9424-01aa75ed71a1/language-en

Eurostat. (2022). *Young people population. Ratio of young people in the total population on 1 January by sex and age [yth_demo_020]*. https://ec.europa.eu/eurostat/databrowser/view/

YTH_DEMO_020__custom_2165280/bookmark/table?lang=en&bookmarkId=9edd0b01-2 6b5-4038-b148-048279e55e2d

Eurostat. (2021). *Statistics on young people neither in employment, nor education or training*. https://ec.europa.eu/eurostat/statisticsexplained/index.php?title=Statistics_on_young_people_ neither_in_employment_nor_in_education_or_training.

Farrugia, D. (2016). The mobility imperative for rural youth: The structural, symbolic and non-representational dimensions rural youth mobilities. *Journal of Youth Studies, 19*(6), 836–851. https://doi.org/10.1080/13676261.2015.1112886

Furlong, A. (2006). Not a very NEET solution: Representing problematic labour market transitions among early school-leavers. Work, Employment and Society, 20(3), 553–569. https://doi.org/ 10.1177/0950017006067001

Gottfredson, L. S. (2002). Gottfredson's theory of circumscription, compromise, and self-creation. In D. Brown (Ed.), *Career choice and development* (pp. 85–148). Jossey-Bass.

International Labour Organization. (2022). *Global employment trends for youth 2022*. https://www.ilo.org/wcmsp5/groups/public/%2D%2D-dgreports/%2D%2D-dcomm/%2D%2D-publ/documents/publication/wcms_853321.pdf

Leibert, T. (2016). She leaves, he stays? Sex-selective migration in rural East Germany. *Journal of Rural Studies, 43*, 267–279. https://doi.org/10.1016/j.jrurstud.2015.06.004

Lent, R. W., Brown, S. D., & Hackett, G. (2000). Contextual supports and barriers to career choice: A social cognitive analysis. *Journal of Counseling Psychology, 47*(1), 36–49. https://doi.org/10.1037/0022-0167.47.1.36

Lindgren, I., Madsen, C. Ø., Hofmann, S., & Melin, U. (2019). Close encounters of the digital kind: A research agenda for the digitalization of public services. *Government Information Quarterly, 36*, 427–436. https://doi.org/10.1016/j.giq.2019.03.002

Mascherini, M. (2019). Origins and future of the concept of NEETs in the European policy agenda. In J. O'Reilly, J. Leschke, R. Ortlieb, M. Seeleib-Kaiser, & P. Villa (Eds.), *Comparing youth transitions in Europe: Joblessness, insecurity, and inequality*. Oxford Press.

Messersmith, E. E., & Schulenberg, J. E. (2008). When can we expect the unexpected? Predicting educational attainment when it differs from previous expectations. *Journal of Social Issues, 64*(1), 195–212. https://doi.org/10.1111/j.1540-4560.2008.00555.x

Mortimer, J. T., Kim, M., Staff, J., & Vuolo, M. (2016). Unemployment, parental help, and self-efficacy during the transition to adulthood. *Work and Occupations, 43*(3), 434–465. https://doi.org/10.1177/0730888416656904

Pastore, F., Quintano, C., & Rocca, A. (2021). Some young people have all the luck! The duration dependence of the school-to-work transition in Europe. *Labour Economics, 1*, 2. https://doi.org/10.1016/j.labeco.2021.101982

Reagan, E. M., Hambacher, E., Schram, T., McCurdy, K., Lord, D., Higginbotham, T., & Fornauf, B. (2019). Place matters: Review of the literature on rural teacher education. *Teaching and Teacher Education, 80*, 83–93. https://doi.org/10.1016/j.tate.2018.12.005

Sadler, K., Akister, J., & Burch, S. (2015). Who are the young people who are not in education, employment or training? An application of the risk factors to a rural area in the UK. *International Social Work, 58*(4), 508–520. https://doi.org/10.1177/0020872813515010

Schoon, I. (2020). Navigating an uncertain labour market in the UK: The role of structure and agency in the transition from school to work. *Annals, 688*, 77–92. https://doi.org/10.1177/0002716220905569

Silva, S. M., & Abrantes, P. (2017). Growing up in Europe's backyard: Researching on education and youth in Portuguese poor suburban settings. In W. T. Pink & G. W. Noblit (Eds.), *Second International Book of International Education* (pp. 1335–1349). Springer International.

Silva, S.M., Silva, A., González, G., Braziene, R. (2021). Learning to leave and to return: Mobility, place, and sense of belonging amongst young people growing up in border and rural regions of mainland Portugal. Sustainability, 13, 9432. https://doi.org/10.3390/su13169432

Simões, F. (submitted). *Rural NEETs hope across the COVID-19 pandemic: A bioecological mapping*

Simões, F. (2022). School to work transition in the Resilience and Recovery Facility framework: Youth oriented active labour market policies under Pillar 6.

Simões, F. (2018). How to involve rural NEET youths in agriculture? Highlights of an untold story. *Community Development, 49*(5), 556–573. https://doi.org/10.1080/15575330.2018.1531899

Simões, F., & Marta, E. (2024, in press). Public Employment Services and Vulnerable Youth in the EU: The Case of Rural NEETs. *Politics and Governance, 12*, 7432. https://doi.org/10.17645/pag.7432

Simões, F., Erdogan, E., Muratovic, M., & Syk, D. (2022). Scrutinising the exceptionalism of young rural NEETs: A bibiliometric review. *Youth & Society, 54*(2S), 8S–28S. https://doi.org/10.7711/07074/0401414181X82X1210104400534

Simões, F., Meneses, A., Luís, R., & Drumonde, R. (2017). NEETs in a rural region of Southern Europe: Perceived self-efficacy, perceived barriers, educational expectations, and vocational expectations. *Journal of Youth Studies, 20*(9), 1109–1126. https://doi.org/10.1080/13676261.2017.1311403

Simões, F., & Rio, N. (2020). How to increase rural NEETs professional involvement in agriculture? The roles of youth representations and vocational training packages improvement. *Journal of Rural Studies, 75*, 9–19. https://doi.org/10.1016/j.jrurstud.2020.02.007

Simões, F., Rocca, A., Rocha, R., Mateus, C., Marta, E., & Tosun, J. (2021). Time to get emotional: Determinants of university students' intentions to return to rural areas. *Sustainability, 13*, 5135. https://doi.org/10.3390/su13095135

Smoter, M. (2022). Outreach practices of public employment services targeted at NEET youth in Poland. *Youth & Society, 54*(2 Suppl), 89S–108S. https://doi.org/10.1177/0044118X211058224

Snyder, C. R. (2000). *Handbook of hope: Theory, measures, and applications*. Academic Press.

Sullivan, K., Perry, L. B., & McConney, A. (2013). How do school resources and academic performance differ across Australia's rural, regional and metropolitan communities? *Australian Educational Researcher, 40*, 353–372. https://doi.org/10.1007/s13384-013-0100-5

Tosun, J., Treib, O., & Francesco, F. (2019). The impact of the European Youth Guarantee on active labour market policies: A convergence analysis. *International Journal of Social Welfare, 28*, 358–368. https://doi.org/10.1111/ijsw.12375

Unay-Gailhard, I., & Simões, F. (2021). Becoming a young farmer in the digital age—An island perspective. *Rural Sociology, 87*(1), 144–185. https://doi.org/10.1111/ruso.12400

Zipin, L., Sellar, S., Brennan, M., & Gale, T. (2015). Educating for futures in marginalized regions: A sociological framework for rethinking and researching aspirations. *Educational Philosophy and Theory, 47*(3), 227–246. https://doi.org/10.1080/00131857.2013.839376

Open Access This chapter is licensed under the terms of the Creative Commons Attribution 4.0 International License (http://creativecommons.org/licenses/by/4.0/), which permits use, sharing, adaptation, distribution and reproduction in any medium or format, as long as you give appropriate credit to the original author(s) and the source, provide a link to the Creative Commons license and indicate if changes were made.

The images or other third party material in this chapter are included in the chapter's Creative Commons license, unless indicated otherwise in a credit line to the material. If material is not included in the chapter's Creative Commons license and your intended use is not permitted by statutory regulation or exceeds the permitted use, you will need to obtain permission directly from the copyright holder.

Chapter 2
Building Bridges: Community-Based Projects for Participation and Social Inclusion of Rural NEETs

Tatiana Ferreira, Adriano Mauro Ellena, Frida Jonsson, Belém Barbosa, Pınar Uyan-Semerci, Emelj Tuna, Giedrė Kvieskienė, Elena Marta, İlkay Unay-Gailhard, and Maria Fernandes-Jesus

T. Ferreira (✉)
School of Education, Polytechnic Institute of Santarém, Santarém, Portugal
e-mail: tatiana.ferreira@ese.ipsantarem.pt

A. M. Ellena · E. Marta
Università Cattolica del Sacro Cuore, Milan, Italy

CERISVICO - Research Centre on Community Development and Organisational Quality of Life, Brescia, Italy
e-mail: adrianomauro.ellena@unicatt.it; elena.marta@unicatt.it

F. Jonsson
Umeå University, Umeå, Sweden
e-mail: frida.jonsson@umu.se

B. Barbosa
University of Porto, Porto, Portugal
e-mail: belem@fep.up.pt

P. Uyan-Semerci
Istanbul Bilgi University, Istanbul, Turkey
e-mail: pinar.uyan@bilgi.edu.tr

E. Tuna
Ss. Cyril and Methodius University of Skopje, Skopje, North Macedonia
e-mail: emelj.tuna@fznh.ukim.edu.mk

G. Kvieskienė
Vytautas Magnus University, Kaunas, Lithuania
e-mail: giedre.kvieskiene@vdu.lt

İ. Unay-Gailhard
Leibniz Institute of Agricultural Development in Transition Economies (IAMO), Leibniz, Germany
e-mail: unaygailhad@iamo.de

M. Fernandes-Jesus
University of Sussex, Brighton, United Kingdom
e-mail: M.Fernandes-Jesus@sussex.ac.uk

© The Author(s) 2024
F. Simões, E. Erdogan (eds.), *NEETs in European rural areas*, SpringerBriefs in Sociology, https://doi.org/10.1007/978-3-031-45679-4_2

Abstract This chapter focuses on factors that facilitate community-based projects for providing effective and sustainable responses to the challenges faced by young people Not in Employment, Education, or Training (NEETs) in rural areas and more specifically to promote their quality of life and social inclusion. In line with Bronfenbrenner's bioecological model (1977, 1979) and considering community-based projects as part of the exosystem, we aim to identify the barriers and constraints faced by projects targeting young NEETs in rural areas. As part of the collaborative research developed by the members of the "WG1—Rural NEETs Social Networks and Social Inclusion" of the Rural NEET Youth Network, we identified five promising community-based projects in Portugal, Italy, Sweden, North Macedonia, and Lithuania and conducted semi-structured interviews with the project coordinators. Our analysis showed that the identified projects take into account the different levels of the bioecological model and the need to involve how young people and local communities. Both these factors are crucial for their success and sustainability over time.

Keywords Rural NEETs · Youth inclusion · Quality of life · Participation · Community-based projects

2.1 Introduction

Young people's participation in the design and implementation of community-based projects is key to ensuring that such interventions are relevant to them. This is particularly important for those Not in Employment, nor in Education or Training (NEET), who often face exclusion and disengagement (Juvonen & Romakkaniemi, 2019). Inspired by Bronfenbrenner's bioecological model (1977, 1979), in this chapter, we look at the factors that facilitate community-based projects that can effectively support NEETs in rural areas in promoting their quality of life and social inclusion. Recognizing community-based projects as part of the exosystem, which encompasses formal and informal structures (such as the neighborhood) that influence people's lives (Bronfenbrenner, 1977; Newman & Newman, 2020), we aimed to identify projects targeting NEETs and the barriers and constraints faced by community-based projects in rural areas. We looked at promising practices, here defined as an 'intervention, program/service, strategy, or policy that shows potential (or 'promise') for developing into a best practice' (Fazal et al., 2017: 387).

While there has been an increased interest in the conditions, factors, and experiences of NEETs, existing research is still limited to the perspective of NEETs in urban areas (Simões et al., 2022a) and lacks a clear focus on NEETs facing unique challenges including limited access to resources, lack of employment opportunities, and geographic isolation in rural areas (Simões et al., 2022b). Furthermore, as youth participation is a key dimension to understanding social inclusion in rural areas (Simões et al., 2022c), more research is needed to examine how and in which conditions community-based projects involve young people not only as "participants" but as active elements in the development of responses that are relevant to them.

How do projects consider the different levels of the bioecological model in the design and implementation? How is the consideration of the different levels of this model related to achieving the goals of the project and making it sustainable over time? How are young people involved in the different stages of the project? We addressed these questions by focusing on the perspectives of those leading and facilitating community-based projects in rural areas. Based on empirical data, we argue that community-based projects providing effective and sustainable responses to the challenges faced by NEETs in rural youth (i.e., promising practices) are projects which facilitate youth participation, the involvement of the local community, the provision of targeted support and resources, and the development of networks and partnerships. The bioecological model (Bronfenbrenner, 1977, 1979) is used as a theoretical lens to look at these dimensions. Additionally, while our starting point is the mesosystem level, which refers to the connections between the different microsystems that an individual is a part of, in this chapter, we seek to look at the networks, relationships, feedback, and interaction mechanisms within and between systems and levels of the bioecological model.

2.1.1 Being NEET in Rural Areas: The Need for Youth Participation

Youth living in rural areas face several challenges related to limited access to education, limited decent and meaningful work opportunities, and increasing gender gaps (Simões et al., 2022b). Scholars have proposed possible strategies to address these challenges by focusing on facilitating environmentally friendly farming practices that help to develop a positive sense of professional identity, particularly among young women, and highlighting innovation capacity in agriculture-relate jobs (Unay-Gailhard & Bojnec, 2021; Unay-Gailhard & Brennan, 2022). Other approaches highlighted the importance of increasing educational and training opportunities overall and not just in the farming sector (Bojnec & Petrescu, 2021; Petrescu et al., 2022).

While such strategies are undoubtedly needed, addressing rural NEETs' needs should also involve looking at how the physical, social, and cultural environments that young people live in contribute to their quality of life from a wider perspective (Ferreira et al., 2023). Such an approach involves looking at subjective and objective indicators of quality of life and well-being, including human health (e.g., physical, psychological), socioeconomic conditions (e.g., territorial, individual), as well as existing educational and employment opportunities (Ellena et al., 2021; WHO, 2012). Participation is often considered an overarching dimension that helps to improve young people's quality of life and promote their social inclusion, being, therefore, a key priority in several European policies (Ferreira et al., 2023).

Nevertheless, past research has suggested that young people do not feel heard by institutions and political actors, and their concerns and needs are often not considered relevant (e.g., Barret & Zani, 2015; Menezes et al., 2012). The feeling of disempowerment and exclusion from participation spheres is particularly high in young people from marginalized contexts and backgrounds (Barret & Zani, 2015), such as those living in rural areas. Participation is, in this sense, a key dimension to ensure the social inclusion of young people in rural, isolated, or deprived areas (Simões et al., 2022b).

Youth participation is best seen as a continuum ranging from mere attempts to manipulate the process from adults (e.g., decoration, tokenism), and consultation to youth-led initiatives (Hart, 1992, 2008). Relevant projects are, thus, those that are truly able to involve young people in the decision-making processes, are youth-initiated and directed, and in which the decisions are shared with adults. In this regard, previous studies have called for more participatory and inclusive contexts and processes when working with young people (e.g., Malafaia & Fernandes-Jesus, in press; Marta et al., 2022). Engaging young people in the design and implementation of projects targeting their needs is particularly needed when looking at the projects aiming at the quality of life and the social inclusion of NEETs in rural areas.

The nature of the initiatives targeting rural NEETs is another important dimension to consider. Local and bottom-up projects seem to facilitate addressing issues that are culturally, socially, and economically rooted within a particular geographical area or community (e.g., Jakes et al., 2015), ensuring that the project targets the challenges faced by the local community (Wildman et al., 2019). If participation in the community is important for people's well-being and quality of life (e.g., Melås et al., 2023; Wilkinson, 1991), there is a need to look at how projects and initiatives targeting rural NEETs can also facilitate and promote their participation and social inclusion. By social inclusion, we mean the "process of individual's self-realization within a society, acceptance, and recognition of one's potential by social institutions, integration (through study, employment, volunteer work or other forms of participation)" (Kovacheva, 2014: 2). Thus, quality of life and social inclusion of NEETs are not possible without supportive institutions and inclusive social networks. The bioecological model (Bronfenbrenner, 1977, 1979) offers us a lens to look at these dimensions from a comprehensive and interrelated perspective. Community-based projects exist within the intersection of multiple institutions, systems, and levels.

2.2 Identifying Community-Based Projects Across Europe: Our Approach

As part of our collaborative work within the WG1: 'Rural NEETs Social Networks and Social Inclusion' of the Rural NEET Youth Network, we mapped community-based projects targeting rural NEETs across Europe. Our methodological approach consisted of two main phases. In phase one, between June and September 2022, we identified community-based projects focused on the social inclusion of NEETs in rural areas across Europe (Ferreira et al., 2023) through the application of an online survey. The survey was developed by WG1 members and comprised questions related to the characteristics, conceptualization, implementation, and evaluation of the community-based projects.

In total, we identified 43 projects from 14 countries across Europe (see Ferreira et al. (2023), for a detailed description of the projects). These projects focused on the social inclusion of young NEETs in rural areas and highlighted the role of young people's participation. Social inclusion and participation measures and policies at European and national levels tend to focus mainly on education and employment dimensions, and our mapping revealed the need to go beyond these categories, considering youth participation as a pathway to and an outcome of social inclusion. The process and results of the mapping phase were fully reported elsewhere (Ferreira et al., 2023).

More detailed information was needed to fully understand the factors and processes facilitating the implementation of the processes. Thus, the second phase of our mapping involved the selection of examples of promising practices that depicted: (a) a clear focus on youth in rural areas; (b) a community-based approach; (c) an orientation towards the engagement of the community; and (d) the existence of local partnerships. Data collection during this phase involved semi-structured interviews with coordinators of community-based projects meeting the above-mentioned criteria. The interview guide covered questions related to project development, sustainability, dissemination, and impact, as well as partnerships, collaboration, and how young people and the local community were involved. Semi-structured interviews were conducted by co-authors in their first languages between March and April 2023. The interviews were audio recorded and then transcribed verbatim (with an average duration of 1.5 h). All personal information gathered was protected with care and confidentiality required by the General Data Protection Regulation (GDPR) and research ethical principles. Participants were informed about the aim of the interview, that their participation was voluntary, and that they could refuse to answer any questions as well as withdraw from or leave the interview at any time without having to give a reason.

In total, five initiatives were included in the second phase. The projects came from Italy, Portugal, North Macedonia, Lithuania, and Sweden. Our analytical procedure was inspired by qualitative content analysis (Bryman, 2016) and guided by our research questions. A few co-authors (Fernandes-Jesus, Ferreira, and Ellena) prepared an analysis grid with a set of categories (e.g., resources/factors that facilitated the project development; strategies used to engage young people; types of partnerships) that was then completed by the co-authors responsible for conducting the interviews (Barbosa, Ellena, Tuna, Jonsson, Kvieskienė). Three co-authors (Ferreira, Ellena, Fernandes-Jesus) were then involved in comparing and contrasting the different responses, which were then checked by all co-authors.

Table 2.1 Selected community-based projects

Name	Status	Target group	Institutions	Funding
Policoro Project Italy	Ongoing	Young NEETs (15–29 years)	National offices of the Italian Episcopal Conference and other Christian-oriented youth associations	Italian Church
À Volta das Conversas Portugal	Ended (03/2021 to 07/2022)	Wider local Community; Youth (15–24 years); Early school leavers	Between (Ass. Entretodos)—network of professionals constituted as a non-profit association	National government funds
Youth up North Sweden	Ongoing	Young people in rural areas	Boden, Dorotea and Arjeplog municipalities	Kamprad Family Foundation and the Stenbeck Foundation
Sustainable Local Wine North Macedonia	Ongoing	Wider local community; Young people in precarious work (20–34 years)	Slow Food Bitolal Macedonia—Local association or community organisation	European funds, Self-funded, Private Company
Youth Home Lithuania	Ongoing	Institutionalised young people in the process of residential autonomy	Turn to the Children—NGO	Own funds

2.2.1 Promising Community-Based Projects

The five initiatives identified below (see Table 2.1) are considered promising practices. Specifically, they are sustainable projects that consider young people's participation as a key dimension in their approaches.

The 'Policoro' project (Italy) [1] was founded in 1995 through a collaboration between three national offices of the Italian Episcopal Conference, and it is still ongoing. It aims to address youth unemployment in Southern Italy as well as in inland and rural areas by offering a 3-year scholarship to young people who want to become community animators and contribute to the development of their communities. Community animators build partnerships with local stakeholders to help vulnerable youngsters enter the labor market by creating concrete activities (e.g., a 3-year training program, during which they receive a scholarship and a work contract; micro-businesses). The project has achieved various outcomes, such as establishing a national network of young individuals, promoting them as a resource for their region, and initiating successful local enterprises and initiatives.

---

[1] https://www.progettopolicoro.it/

The 'À volta das conversas' (Portugal) [2] project aimed to promote the well-being of young people through the development of their social and emotional skills that can be mobilized to prevent mental health problems, encouraging their collective organization and action as a group and strengthening their mutual support and resilience. The voluntary participation of young people in the project allowed for the identification of problems, the selection of appropriate actions, and the implementation of solutions from a bottom-up perspective, resulting in the creation of a series of impactful activities within their community. In terms of individual impact, the young people developed essential skills and were empowered, which helped them to improve their self-esteem.

'Youth up North' (Sweden) [3] is a 3-year initiative launched in 2020 to build long-term, systemic, and sustainable change in rural areas at the municipal level. The initiative focuses on empowering young people and promoting their entrepreneurial spirit, creativity, and innovation. It also aims to create cross-sector collaborations between civil society, business, and municipalities to shift power relations at a local level, allowing young people to influence their local community. This initiative has resulted in positive outcomes such as the employment of youth coordinators, the establishment of local youth clubs, and the inclusion of youth participation in the political agenda of municipalities.

The 'Youth Home' project (Lithuania) [4] developed by the 'Turn to the Children' organization started in 2016. It aims at providing social care services and psychosocial assistance to young people who have lost parental care as well as employment services to those growing up in social-risk families to help them to be prepared for independent living. Assessments were carried out, and participants gave positive feedback about the project, thus becoming promoters of the project within the community.

Finally, the 'Sustainable Local Wine' project (North Macedonia) [5] aimed to support young wine producers to stay or return to rural areas. The project impacts include direct and indirect benefits for young farmers and for the agricultural sector overall, as well as contributions to the sustainability of rural areas. The project offered opportunities for training, investment planning, and marketing strategies to young people, motivating them to either continue their family's wine production or pursue studies in enology to innovate in the field.

Overall, these five projects represent promising practices of community-based projects who have put youth participation at the heart of their action. They were implemented in quite different contexts and with different goals. Nevertheless, they share some common aspects discussed in the following sections.

---

[2] https://www.between.pt/projetos/a-volta-das-conversas

[3] https://flyttatillboden.se/en/a-countryside-where-young-people-want-to-live/

[4] https://atsigrezk.lt/seimynos/jaunimo-namai

[5] http://www.slowfood.mk/

2.2.2 Contextually Grounded Projects

Our interviewees highlighted local-based, tailored, and individualized approaches, which are considered to be strengths and distinctive aspects of these projects. Whilst these projects were developed based on the identification of contextual needs, European and national policies, and measures have helped to create the conditions and access to the resources needed for the implementation of these projects. For example, the 'Youth Home' was described as a project aligned and inspired by national policies, but the access to structural funding was key in its initial implementation phases. Nevertheless, the approach to the project was very much adapted and inspired by lived experiences, training, and knowledge of those involved. Similarly, the 'Sustainable Local Wine' project was designed following new legislation in North Macedonia, which has facilitated the development of the project. In a way, this project caught the wave or the period when the law for spreading wineries across the country was enforced, and this was an actual opportunity for practical implementation of the factual changes in the Law. Conversely, the changes in the law directly influenced the success of the project. Thus, even when the projects are funded within a policy and are aligned with European and national priorities, they seem to follow other sources of inspiration and are often developed based on the identification of needs and funding in a way that supports these needs.

The 'Policoro' and the 'À volta das conversas' are two interesting examples of projects that were not driven by top-down measures and interventions. According to the interviewee from the 'Policoro' project, this initiative was completely bottom-up and grounded in local needs:

> The project is not specifically coordinated with national or regional policies. It stands as a parallel alternative to other measures and interventions. However, its strength lies in being extremely rooted in the local community and territory by providing tailor-made designs. In this context, it dialogues with different institutions, including municipal ones, while establishing a collaborative partnership (Policoro, Italy).

Likewise, 'À volta das conversas' has developed its methodology inspired by the 'Children's Parliaments', a methodology that aims to facilitate children's rights and participation (Tolson, 2022). This project invested in strong partnership-building with local institutions and experts on the topic of mental health and created spaces for youth participation. Additionally, while there is a lack of measures and policies targeting rural areas (Petrescu et al., 2022), the 'Youth Up North' project provides an example of how local organizations are addressing rural challenges without the existence of national policies directed towards young people in rural areas or rural NEETs. However, to achieve the aim of contributing to long-term, systemic, and sustainable change *with* and *for* young people in the Swedish rural inland, the change processes of the 'Youth Up North' have been deliberately integrated into existing and established municipal structures. One specific example of such integration is the establishment of a youth coordinator, one young person from the local community who has been employed by the municipality to promote change in line with the needs and wishes of their peers.

2.2.3 Centering on Youth Participation

While each project depicts unique characteristics, they all represent a significant attempt to engage young people both in the design and implementation phases as well as in peer-to-peer activities. In the 'Policoro' project, young people are involved as community animators and as beneficiaries of the activities. Community animators are proposed and selected locally. Afterward, they are engaged in the training and design process involving other young people through building a relationship of trust based on a peer-to-peer learning approach. Although a strong involvement of young people was also foreseen in the 'À volta das conversas' project, their participation was more prominent during the various planning stages, and young people were also involved in developing the methodology. This project is described as a continuous process of planning, implementation, and evaluation, and young people provide feedback that is taken into consideration to improve the methodology. This methodology places participation as its main dimension, and the project's vision is "to hold this space for participation and at the same time allow the participants themselves to become potential facilitators of the participatory space." (À volta das conversas, Portugal). Participation is then an outcome of the project, but also the means throughout the project is developed (Rosa & Fernandes-Jesus, 2021).

Similarly, the 'Youth Home' and 'Youth Up North' projects highlighted the engagement of young people in the design, implementation, and dissemination of the project. For example, 'Youth Up North' followed an interactive four-step model inspired by a youth-centered approach that involved co-creation with youth and adult stakeholders. The initiative evolved, shifting from focusing mainly on the inclusion and influence of young people to challenging the ageism of adult-centric discourse and practices that actively exclude them. As part of this approach, one of the young participants is employed by the municipality and serves as a point of reference for their peers. A different approach was taken by the 'Sustainable Local Wine' project, which seems to have involved young people mainly in the implementation phase of the project. Nevertheless, young people were also instrumental in mobilizing, activating, and motivating other young people to participate in developing the necessary changes pursued by the project.

The ability to create generative partnerships and intense community involvement were very salient strengths of these projects. For the "Policoro" project, this factor was essential, as the community animators had the tasks of being present in the community and involving all associations and institutions in the planning of concrete activities: 'One of the strategies that have been used over the years, which has also been very successful, is to be present as community animators within the various realities that constitute the community.' (Policoro, Italy).

Interestingly, the 'Youth Up North' initiative has also focused on supporting cross-sector collaborations locally between civil society, business, and the municipality, as well as intergenerational collaborations between young people and local/regional discussion-makers. The 'À volta das conversas' involved schools and NGOs with expertise on the subject as partners. Involvement of the extended community and families was envisaged in the project but, unfortunately, not fully feasible due to the Covid-19 pandemic. The involvement of the youth's families and related support institutions (e.g., schools, employment services, companies, and municipalities) was key for the 'Youth Home' project. Equally important was the involvement of the municipality and experienced local consultants. Finally, in 'Sustainable Local Wine' numerous partners were involved, although mainly related to the agricultural sector of interest.

2.2.4 Facing Barriers and Constraints

Based on our analysis, these projects have encountered three types of barriers and obstacles. The first one includes barriers associated with the lack of motivation and interest from young people, who are described as being in psychological distress and lacking the will to be engaged. According to our interviewees, this is due to some extent to a lack of confidence in their abilities and partly associated with a lack of trust in the system and institutions. This issue is particularly evident in three out of the five projects ('Policoro', 'À volta das conversa' and 'Youth Up North'): "Some of them [young people] were very disengaged and had low self-esteem, many fears, and a lack of motivation. Initially, it was challenging to engage them because they were skeptical and disbelieving." (À volta das conversas, Portugal).

Another type of barrier is related to the social representations that young people have about rural areas. Rural areas are not seen as attractive to young people such as urban areas (Unay-Gailhard & Brennan, 2022; Unay-Gailhard & Bojnec, 2021), which contributes to many of them refusing the idea of being involved in community-based initiatives and further blocking their participation in these projects. For instance, the 'Youth Up North' project highlighted this sort of social barriers when trying to engage young people locally in the municipalities. The negative images and discourses of rural residents and of rural areas as socially homogeneous were described as having a direct implication in the way young people engaged in the change process by censoring or limiting themselves: "Young people are so pragmatic in the inland that it becomes boring to have visionary workshops because the young people stop themselves so early in the imaginary process." (Youth Up North, Sweden). This was also highlighted by the 'Sustainable Local Wine' project, which encountered young people enrolled in traditional agricultural practices who also lacked the motivation to move ahead with their ideas.

A third type of barrier relates to the lack of resources and supporting institutions, such as schools. This is again well-explained by the Swedish project. Most of the inland municipalities of the Swedish north do not have an upper secondary school, meaning that young people typically either leave or commute for many hours a day to go to school, making it very difficult to reach the school precinct:

> Then we can talk about those who don't go to school, the NEETs, but we must also remember that in [location] there is no high school. So, most of the young people move away when they are 15 years old, and they have been incredibly difficult to reach. So, I

would say that our challenge in terms of age has been that as soon as young people do not have a natural place, such as a school to go to, it is very difficult for a project like this to reach them. (Youth Up North, Sweden).

Overall, the barriers identified by participants are more often structural and related to the lack of resources that facilitate young people's engagement with community-based projects. Even the lack of interest and motivation is described as being associated with a lack of opportunities in rural areas, which further explains disengagement.

2.2.5 Sustaining the Project over Time

The five projects shared a keen interest in finding solutions that would ensure the sustainability of activities and enable participants to carry them out by themselves. The key factor in achieving this sustainability is the ability to build partnerships with various stakeholders within the community. For example, in the 'Policoro' project, the sustainability of the proposed activities is ensured by the strong alliances with the local entities involved as well as by the presence of the community animator, should they wish to do so after 3 years. Similarly, the 'À volta com as conversas' is strongly orientated towards the project continuity and sustainability, and that is why the project also seeks to involve school teachers and train young people to take over the leadership and facilitation of the project. Despite the initial low participation, the impact of some community activities attracted young people in the following year, allowing the project to continue to exist autonomously without the involvement of the organization that implemented the project in the first place.

Furthermore, the 'Sustainable Local Wine' project suggested that partnerships and involvement of professional experts and volunteers were critical to ensuring the project's sustainability over time, more than financial resources. Similarly, interinstitutional cooperation was essential to the success of the 'Youth Home' project, which involved schools, companies, mental health centers, and other organizations in the project. Partnerships with private and international stakeholders, such as the Norwegian Lions Club, were important to guarantee the quality and regularity of salaries for the technicians involved in the project: "Inter-institutional cooperation is of great value because by consolidating it, we can create a support network for young people and more productively solve the difficulties that have arisen in the life path of young people." (Youth Home, Lithuania). The creation of the steering group in the 'Youth Up North' project also encouraged policymakers to talk about young people's participation and facilitated the development of the project over time.

> We have gathered some of the municipalities' top decision-makers, who are forced to every two months have two hours in their calendar every day to talk about young people's influence. That, I think, has created a lot of ripple effects, which was not our idea from the beginning, but was more of a necessity. (Youth Up North, Sweden)

Importantly, as highlighted in the previous quote, such space was important to overcome the barriers faced by the project, contributing to its sustainability over time.

2.3 Conclusion

In this chapter, we have looked at community-based projects and how they facilitate the social inclusion and participation of rural NEET youth. Taking the bioecological model as a lens, we conclude that these selected projects take into account the different levels of the bioecological model and that the barriers mentioned are partly related to the difficulties in mobilizing interactions between different levels (e.g., supporting institutions) (Trickett & Rowe, 2012).

Furthermore, our analysis suggests that the most sustainable projects are those that are tailored and locally based. The local dimension of the community-based projects was associated with greater community engagement and youth participation (Malafaia & Fernandes-Jesus, in press; Marta et al., 2022). These projects are alternatives to other existing initiatives in the community, seeking to fill the gaps created by the mass responses of policies designed at a macro level without considering the specificities of the local context.

The ability to create and consolidate partnerships (e.g., intergenerational collaborations, extended community and families; supportive environment by institutions such as schools and municipalities) is one of the greatest strengths and potentials of the analyzed projects and the one that creates the best conditions for its implementation and sustainability over time.

To ensure such sustainability, it is necessary to consider the different levels of the bioecological model and, importantly, how they relate to each other. Therefore, it is essential to consider the exosystem (e.g., social networks, community support institutions, etc.), as well as how the elements within this level interact with the different levels.

Indeed, the continuous and collaborative dialogue with different public and private institutions is indeed a transversal feature of all five projects, demonstrating the importance of local support systems and institutions to promote social inclusion and quality of life (Kovacheva, 2014). The projects also revealed the importance of developing local and bottom-up initiatives that are rooted in the cultural, social, and economic specificities of the community (Jakes et al., 2015; Wildman et al., 2019), complementing top-down national interventions that provide standardized responses that are not culturally and contextually grounded in a territory. However, European/national policies and measures help to create the conditions that facilitate access to the resources needed to implement projects (e.g., Youth Home; Sustainable Local Wine).

The five projects describe several attempts to engage young people in both the design and implementation phases and to facilitate peer-to-peer activities. In this regard, the community-based projects highlighted the need for youth-led projects to avoid the adult-centered vision of project development in which younger generations are often regarded as mere beneficiaries (Ferreira et al., 2023; Malafaia & Fernandes-Jesus, in press).

A number of structural barriers and barriers related to the lack of resources and opportunities in rural areas were identified as hindering young people's participation in the projects. Firstly, the lack of motivation and interest of young people is linked with a lack of confidence in their abilities and/or a lack of trust in the system and institutions (e.g. Policoro; À Volta das Conversas; Youth Up Nrorth). The second type of barrier is related to the image of rural areas, which are not considered attractive for young people, and to the lack of motivation for traditional agricultural practices. Finally, the third barrier is related to the lack of resources and supporting institutions.

In conclusion, the projects we have discussed demonstrate the importance of combining the local dimension with the centrality of young people's participation as a way of overcoming barriers and sustaining the project over time. In light of our findings, effectively engaging rural NEETs in community-based projects is complex and the factors contributing to these challenges are multi-faceted.

An important limitation of our study is the convenience sampling approach used, but given that we were not interested in best- or good-practices, we are confident that these five projects are examples of promising practices. An additional limitation of our work is that we emphasize only the perspective of adults involved in community-based projects targeting rural young NEETs.

2.3.1 New Research Developments

Our results highlighted the importance of rethinking the way research agendas are defined, not only upstream, in the definition of priority lines of funding at different scales—European, national, and local, but also downstream, in the process of design, implementation, and evaluation of processes, through some key actions.

- **Involving rural NEETs in research.** Young people should be involved in research processes: (a) in the definition of funding priorities, in order to meet their needs and expectations and (b) in the different stages of project development, from design to implementation and evaluation, in order to overcome the adult-centric vision which often characterizes research on young people. *Research should focus on the voices and perspectives of rural NEETs and involve young people as co-researchers or support and fund youth-led initiatives and projects.*
- **Connecting and building bridges within the community.** Our analysis of five different projects has shown the importance of community involvement and how it can increase the impact of projects in the territory. These bridges, mobilizing and linking local resources and partnerships, allow projects to respond to the problems, needs, opportunities, and specific potential of each territorial context.

In this process, it is also important to promote the participation of young people in planning and defining what is important for their communities. *Research should consider a participatory diagnostic phase involving local actors.*
- **Taking into account the diversity and plurality of the youth condition.** Top-down programs and priority agendas are based on and reproduce a uniform and homogeneous vision of what it means to be young. Our findings highlight the importance of assessing community-based projects, rooted in the territory, that promote young people's participation and social inclusion through a more personalized and tailor-made approach, focusing on the diverse profiles of young people. *Research should go beyond the one-size-fits-all view of youth and take into account its pluralities in terms of gender, ethnicity, place of residence (urban/rural), migration background, etc.*
- **Exploring further the bioecological model framework.** Research should also seek to build a more comprehensive analysis by looking at the different levels of the bioecological model rather than just focusing on the perspective of individuals, institutions, or policies. Given our findings, effectively engaging rural NEETs in community-based projects is complex, and the factors contributing to these challenges are multilayered. *Research should, therefore, consider exploring the different layers of the bioecological model.*

2.3.2 Policy Recommendations

In terms of policy recommendations, our results inform approaches to rural NEETs that are grounded on their needs and active involvement. Specifically, we recommend that:

- **Considering the differences between EU Members.** European policies implementation. In the European context, projects should consider the range of cultural and socioeconomic differences among EU Member States where rural youth experience different forms of rurality (Bæck, 2016).
- **Developing local and bottom-up projects.** The projects covered by our research efforts revealed the importance of developing local and bottom-up projects that are rooted in the cultural, social, and economic singularities of each community (Jakes et al., 2015; Wildman et al., 2019), contrasting with the top-down a-specific national interventions that offer standardized responses, not culturally and contextually grounded in a territory.
- **Foster partnerships.** Establishing partnerships is crucial for the implementation and sustainability of the project over time. To ensure such sustainability, there is a need to consider the different levels of the bioecological model and, importantly, how they relate to each other. Therefore, while it is essential to consider the exosystem (e.g., social networks, community support institutions, etc.), it is also key to look at how the elements within this level interact with the different levels proposed by the bioecological model (from micro to macro).

References

Bæck, U. D. K. (2016). Rural location and academic success – remarks on research, contextualisation and methodology. *Scandinavian Journal of Educational Research, 60*(4), 435–448. https://doi.org/10.1080/00313831.2015.1024163

Barrett, M., & Zani, B. (2015). *Political and civic engagement: Multidisciplinary perspectives*. Routledge.

Bojnec, S., & Petrescu, C. (2021). *Youth policy – application of the intervention: Best practices with rural Neets*. COST Action CA 18213. https://rnyobservatory.eu/web/wp-content/uploads/2022/04/book-application-intervention-rural-neets.pdf

Bronfenbrenner, U. (1977). Toward an experimental ecology of human development. *American Psychologist, 32*(7), 513–531. https://doi.org/10.1037/0003-066X.32.7.513

Bronfenbrenner, U. (1979). *The ecology of human development: Experiments by nature and design*. Harvard University Press.

Bryman, A. (2016). *Social research methods* (5th ed.). Oxford University Press.

Ellena, A. M., Marta, E., Simões, F., Fernandes-Jesus, M., & Petrescu, C. (2021). Soft skills and psychological well-being: A study on Italian rural and urban NEETs. *Calitatea Vieții, 32*(4), 352–370. https://doi.org/10.46841/RCV.2021.04.02

Fazal, N., Jackson, S. F., Wong, K., Yessis, J., & Jetha, N. (2017). Between worst and best: Developing criteria to identify promising practices in health promotion and disease prevention for the Canadian best practices portal. *Health Promotion and Chronic Disease Prevention in Canada: Research, Policy and Practice, 37*(11), 386–392. https://doi.org/10.24095/hpcdp.37.11.03

Ferreira, T., Ellena, A. M., Fernandes-Jesus, M., Jonsson, F., Barbosa, B., Tuna, E., Silva, V. C., Marta, E., Muratović, M., Semerci, P., Erdogan, E., Emirhafizović, M., Vieira, M. M., Rosa, M. C., Kvieskienė, G., Kvieska, V., Querol, V., Brumovska, T., & Nasya, B. (2023). *Mapping community-based projects promoting participation and social inclusion of youth NEETs in rural areas across Europe*. COST Action CA 18213. https://rnyobservatory.eu/web/wp-content/uploads/2023/03/REPORT-WG1-Mapping-Community-Based-Projects-Promoting.pdf

Hart, R. (1992). *Children's participation: From tokenism to citizenship*. UNICEF Innocenti Essays, No. 4, International Child Development Centre of UNICEF.

Hart, R. A. (2008). Stepping back from 'The Ladder': Reflections on a model of participatory work with children. In A. Reid, B. B. Jensen, J. Nikel, & V. Simovska (Eds.), *Participation and learning* (pp. 19–31). Springer. https://doi.org/10.1007/978-1-4020-6416-6_2

Jakes, S., Hardison-Moody, A., Bowen, S., & Blevins, J. (2015). Engaging community change: The critical role of values in asset mapping. *Community Development, 46*(4), 392–406. https://doi.org/10.1080/15575330.2015.1064146

Juvonen, T., & Romakkaniemi, M. (2019). Between mobility and belonging: The meanings of locality among youth in Lapland in the transition to adulthood. *Young, 27*(4), 321–335. https://doi.org/10.1177/1103308818791672

Kovacheva, S. (2014). *EU-CoE Youth partnership policy sheet. social inclusion*. EU-CoE youth partnership. http://pjp-eu.coe.int/pt/web/youth-partnership/social-inclusion

Malafaia, C., & Fernandes-Jesus, M. (in press). Youth climate activism: Addressing research pitfalls and centring young people's voices. In A. Carvalho & T. R. Peterson (Eds.), *Handbook of environmental communication*. De Gruyter Mouton.

Marta, E., Ellena, A. M., Marzana, D., Corrado, C., Nadia, V., & Antonella, R. (2022). People beyond NEETs: A person – and territory-centred approach to combating social exclusion. In S. Bojnec & C. Petrescu (Eds.), *COST CA18213 Rural NEET Youth policy brief – application of the intervention: Best-practices with rural NEETs* (pp. 113–135). https://rnyobservatory.eu/web/wp-content/uploads/2022/04/book-application-intervention-rural-neets.pdf

Melås, A., Farstad, M., & Frisvoll, S. (2023). Rural youth: Quality of life, civil participation and outlooks for a rural future. In P. H. Johansen, A. Tietjen, E. B. Iversen, H. L. Lolle, & J. K.

Fisker (Eds.), *Rural quality of life* (pp. 258–273). Manchester University Press. https://doi.org/10.7765/9781526161642

Menezes, I., Ribeiro, N., Fernandes-Jesus, M., Malafaia, C., & Ferreira, P. (Eds.). (2012). *Agência e participação cívica e política: jovens e imigrantes na construção da democracia*. Livpsic.

Newman, B. M., & Newman, P. R. (2020). *Theories of adolescent development*. Academic Press. https://doi.org/10.1016/C2017-0-03324-4

Petrescu, C., Ellena, A. M., Fernandes-Jesus, M., & Marta, E. (2022). Using evidence in policies addressing rural NEETs: Common patterns and differences in various EU countries. *Youth & Society, 54*(2_Suppl), 69S–88S. https://doi.org/10.1177/0044118X211056361

Rosa, M. C., & Fernandes-Jesus, M. (2021). "Círculos de Cidadania" para uma cidadania global: um programa de intervenção para a promoção da participação cívica de crianças. *Revista Sinergias, 11*, 91–108. http://sinergiased.org/index.php/revista/item/300

Simões, F., Erdoğan, E., Muratović, M., & Sik, D. (2022a). Scrutinising the exceptionalism of young rural NEETs: A bibliometric review. *Youth & Society, 54*(2_Suppl), 8S–28S. https://doi.org/10.1177/0044118X211040534

Simões, F., Fernandes-Jesus, M., & Marta, E. (2022b). NEETs civic and political participation in outermost islands: The mediating roles of sense of community and agency. *Journal of Community & Applied Social Psychology, 32*(5), 799–813. https://doi.org/10.1002/casp.2609

Simões, F., Fernandes-Jesus, M., Marta, E., Albanesi, C., & Carr, N. (2022c). The increasing relevance of European rural young people in policy agendas: Contributions from community psychology. *Community & Applied Social Psychology, 33*(1), 3–13. https://doi.org/10.1002/casp.2640

Tolson, E. (2022). *Weaving global governance from below: Neighbourocracy and children's parliaments in India*. https://www.sociocracyforall.org/childrens-parliaments-sociocracy-case-study/

Trickett, E. J., & Rowe, H. L. (2012). Emerging ecological approaches to prevention, health promotion, and public health in the school context: Next steps from a community psychology perspective. *Journal of Educational and Psychological Consultation, 22*(1–2), 125–140. https://doi.org/10.1080/10474412.2011.649651

Unay-Gailhard, İ., & Bojnec, S. (2021). Gender and the environmental concerns of young farmers: Do young women farmers make a difference on family farms? *Journal of Rural Studies, 88*, 71–82. https://doi.org/10.1016/j.jrurstud.2021.09.027

Unay-Gailhard, İ., & Brennan, M. A. (2022). How digital communications contribute to shaping the career paths of youth: A review study focused on farming as a career option. *Agriculture and Human Values, 39*(4), 1491–1508. https://doi.org/10.1007/s10460-022-10335-0

WHO – World Health Organization. (2012). *The world health organization quality of life (WHOQOL)*. https://www.who.int/publications/i/item/WHO-HIS-HSI-Rev.2012.03

Wildman, J. M., Valtorta, N., Moffatt, S., & Hanratty, B. (2019). 'What works here doesn't work there': The significance of local context for a sustainable and replicable asset-based community intervention aimed at promoting social interaction in later life. *Health & Social Care in the Community, 27*(4), 1102–1110. https://doi.org/10.1111/hsc.12735

Wilkinson, K. P. (1991). *The community in rural America*. Social Ecology Press.

Open Access This chapter is licensed under the terms of the Creative Commons Attribution 4.0 International License (http://creativecommons.org/licenses/by/4.0/), which permits use, sharing, adaptation, distribution and reproduction in any medium or format, as long as you give appropriate credit to the original author(s) and the source, provide a link to the Creative Commons license and indicate if changes were made.

The images or other third party material in this chapter are included in the chapter's Creative Commons license, unless indicated otherwise in a credit line to the material. If material is not included in the chapter's Creative Commons license and your intended use is not permitted by statutory regulation or exceeds the permitted use, you will need to obtain permission directly from the copyright holder.

Chapter 3
Rural NEETs: Pathways Through Formal and Non-formal Education

Paul Flynn, Heidi Paabort, Valentina Milenkova, Katerina Bojkovska, Antonella Rocca, Liena Hačatrjana, Vladislava Lendzhova, Albena Nakova, and Marta de Oliveira Rodrigues

Abstract Formal and non-formal education often constitute the first line of engagement in supporting Rural young people Not in Employment, nor in Education, or Training (NEET). However, it is not always the case that such interventions are widely documented. This chapter aims to uncover best practice interventions for the educational inclusion of rural NEETs building upon an emergent body of work in order to frame the identification of five case studies across Estonia, Italy, Latvia, Albania, Portugal. EU and non-EU member states were included to offer a diverse set of examples. Based on Bronfenbrenner's bioecological model and data triangulation, elements that prevent rural youth from entering or staying in NEET status were identified. Our work shows that each formal or nonformal education learning intervention or reform mobilizes different levels of the bioecological framework and has an important function in shaping NEETs or at-risk youth support systems. Educational interventions that directly target young people can improve the

P. Flynn (✉)
University of Galway, Galway, Ireland
e-mail: PAUL.FLYNN@nuigalway.ie

H. Paabort
Estonian Social Insurance Board, University of Tartu, Tartu, Estonia

V. Milenkova · V. Lendzhova
South-West University "Neofit Rilsky", Blagoevgrad, Bulgaria

K. Bojkovska
St. Kliment Ohridski University, Sofia, North Macedonia

A. Rocca
University of Naples Parthenope, Naples, Italy

L. Hačatrjana
Faculty of Pedagogy, Psychology and Arts, University of Latvia, Riga, Latvia

A. Nakova
Institute of Philosophy and Sociology, Sofia, Bulgaria

M. de Oliveira Rodrigues
Faculty of Psychology and Education Sciences, University of Porto, Porto, Portugal

© The Author(s) 2024
F. Simões, E. Erdogan (eds.), *NEETs in European rural areas*, SpringerBriefs in Sociology, https://doi.org/10.1007/978-3-031-45679-4_3

likelihood of a positive outcome when they are context specific. In addition, these interventions make it possible to see the potential of different educational methods in supporting rural young people, when that contextualization stems directly from the young person's perspectives and his/her perceived needs.

Keywords NEET · Rural youth · Bronfenbrenner's Bioecological Model · Best practices intervention · Formal education · Non-formal education

3.1 Introduction

Formal and non-formal education pathways have a crucial role to play in preventing rural youth from becoming and remaining not in Employment, nor in Education or Training (NEET). The school-to-work transition is complex as are the multi-layered actions that impact that environment such as macrosystem policy, mesosystem-level governance, and microsystem-level aiming at these young people's engagement with education. Foundational issues for the success of these interventions include (a) rural education infrastructure and human resources that support the school-to-work transition; (b) mapping non-formal education aimed at vulnerable young people in rural areas, in terms of existing infrastructures, types of organization, and types of interventions; (c) the role of Vocational Education and Training (VET) in preventing Early School Leaving from Education and Training (ESLET) in rural areas; and (d) analyzing how the available curricula address local resources and map onto the needs of these young people. This chapter will present a contextualization of the aforementioned issues, thus providing a heretofore much-needed characterization of the naturalistic context of educational provision targeted at rural NEETs in Europe.

To conduct our analysis, we focus on Bronfenbrenner's Bioecological Model, which constitutes a theoretical framework for understanding the complex relationship between rural NEET young people and their environment, at various levels (macrosystem, exosystem, mesosystem, and microsystem), with a direct impact on the development of these young people (Bronfenbrenner, 1999). In line with this theoretical framework, we present a multiple case study from five countries (Estonia, Italy, Latvia, Albania, and Portugal) based on a qualitative approach. Each intervention is developed in the context of national or EU programs in formal and non-formal education settings. The results of the work of Petrescu et al. (2020) and Erdogan et al. (2022) enabled the identification and characterization of five best practice interventions. We feature such interventions here as macro, meso, and micro-level interventions that are present for adoption in cognate contexts: (1) macro-level (EU or state-level interventions, top-down actions, that may include reforms); (2) meso-level (regional or networked coordinated interventions that are influenced or informed by the macro-level, actions that inform local or small-scale interventions) and; (3) micro-level (localized activities that are effective in their own environment, community engagement projects that may have potential for bottom-up reforms). The establishment of COST Action Rural NEET Youth Network

Working Group 2, which seeks to understand the educational challenges that NEETs face in rural settings, has resulted in a critical mass of researchers focused on this area. We seek to present an insight into the reflexive relationship that is needed between the three levels, identifying some commonalities that can help to arrest the prevalence of young people from entering or staying in the NEET status in rural areas where ESLET is more prevalent (Eurostat, 2020). Finally, some general recommendations are outlined which suggest actions that may benefit rural NEET engagement with formal or non-formal educational interventions.

3.2 Supporting Macro-level Educational Interventions

When thinking about educational interventions, Bronfenbrenner's bioecological model draws a theoretical framework for understanding the complex interplay between human development and environmental factors focusing on the agentic role of individual development (Guy-Evans, 2020). At the macrosystem level, the bioecological model can support education and school-to-work transition by examining the broader cultural, social, economic, and political systems as elements that can make a meaningful contribution to education (Bronfenbrenner, 1999; Bronfenbrenner & Evans, 2000). An important contribution of Bronfenbrenner's model at the macrosystem level is that it helps us to understand the reflexive relationship between education and the cultural and social values that form the holistic perspective of education by those that inform the sector and participate within it. The model is also crucial in how we determine extant and emergent barriers in the connection between the social context and the education systems. It is this connectivity that the model allows which can play a key role in supporting policy change and analyzing economic and political systems for the benefit of European citizenship in general (INSTAT, 2021). These contributions of the bioecological model are summarized in Fig. 3.1.

Understanding the cultural and social values is a key element shaping educational systems in rural areas and when considering how an educational intervention might offer opportunities for rural NEETs in particular. The value placed on education and the belief in any educational system by those who are disengaged from education and training pathways are important elements for composing educational policies that might shape educational practices. The consideration of these values at the macrosystem level when thinking about how policy can impact the role of educators and trainers in rural settings. An absence of connectivity to such values can only hinder their expectation to align their efforts with the needs of rural students especially when designing teaching methods and curricula.

Based on this, cultural and social values in rural areas have a critical influence on the availability of opportunities for individual citizens to learn and develop skills (Simões et al., 2022). Therefore it is important that the design and delivery of educational programs embrace these cultural and social factors that affect NEETs living in rural areas if the overall incidence rate of rural NEETs is to be reduced

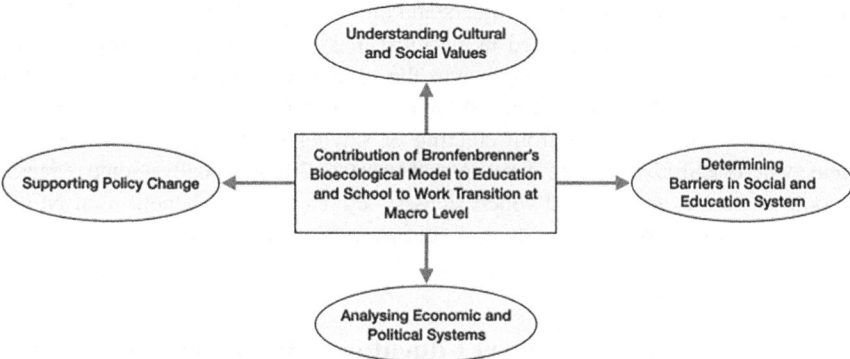

Fig. 3.1 Contributions of Bronfenbrenner's bioecological model to education and school-to-work transition at the macrosystem

(Cabinet of Ministers Republic of Latvia, 2021). From the bioecological model perspective, at the macrosystem level, cultural norms, laws, and social policies shape the opportunities and constraints of individuals. Therefore, the development of policies and curricula at the macrosystem level will have an important impact on the school-to-work transition and educational attainment level of rural NEETs in key areas such as (a) improvement of the educational conditions of both teachers and students; (b) provision of targeted incentives to rural NEETs to engage them with educational programs; (c) meaningful and situated training curricula relevant to rural youth; (d) improved regulations for professional development; and (e) development of policies that concomitantly improve social and educational facilities in rural settings. In order to meet these pillars, interventions operating at the macrosystem must include a detailed analysis of the country's political and educational system and how they can specifically address rural NEETs. Given rural NEETs are in a disadvantaged group and experience a greater need for the distribution of resources and opportunities within society than other demographic groups, it is vital that actors at the macrosystem level identify the challenges faced in contemporaneous situations and take measures for the development of both educators and students which are duly informed by the lived experience of rural NEETs. In such a way, the practices, education system, teaching methods, and all components of education will be framed and shaped by the political and educational system at the macrosystem level—meaning they are connected (INSTAT, 2021). Policy reforms that target rural NEETs are well illustrated in Italy, presented in Box 3.1.

Box 3.1 Educational policy reforms at the macrosystem: example from Italy

> In Italy, Law 107 was adopted in 2015 to make secondary education less theoretical and closer to what the labor market requires. The main goal of this

(continued)

> school reform was to integrate the school pathway of students with greater knowledge about and experience of career practices. The law consists of the provision of additional hours in the compulsory school program to be organized in coordination with factories and institutions, and consisting of practical courses on the activities usually performed in the workplace. Since its introduction, there are significant signs of progress in terms of the improvement of school programs. Also, many schools have created education committees composed of teachers and experts in the labor market, professional representatives, and scientific and technological units. These scientific committees are expected to enforce the connections between the school's educational objectives, the needs of local communities where schools are located, and the professional needs of the local labor markets (Rocca, 2023).

While the aforementioned considerations are necessary to improve the condition of rural NEETs and such action must occur at the macrosystem level, barriers to getting this work done are prevalent. Stagnant political system processes hinder the capacity of any willing and empowered educational system to ameliorate the challenges faced by NEETs and to aid efforts to reach them. However, an application of Bronfenbrenner's Bioecological model can help identify such systemic barriers for rural NEETs access to formal and non-formal education. These include, as we have seen in previous chapters, gender disparities, poor socioeconomic conditions (Simões, 2023), or lower levels of civic and social participation, due to a limited number of opportunities to do so that disproportionately affect vulnerable rural young people (Tatiana et al., 2023). Examining and assessing these barriers will help managers and educators to create a more equitable, tailored, and inclusive educational system. Presently, the absence of a comprehensive framework to support youth development through the identification of systemic problems is a challenge in and of itself for macrosystem level actors such as policymakers, educators, and other stakeholders within education systems. The employment of Bronfenbrenner's model could provide an opportunity for targeted reforms as part of larger cultural and social contexts. Taking this approach, NEETs' individual opportunities and experiences can be demonstrably improved by including values, beliefs, norms, and habits within macro-level decision-making processes thus offering the potential to challenge the discrimination that NEETs face based on race, ethnicity, gender, or sexual orientation.

Bronfenbrenner's bioecological model can also support policy innovation and development by highlighting the systemic factors that influence the education and training of NEETs in rural areas, including knowing and reaching out to young people. Policy innovation in outreaching rural NEETs is well illustrated by the Estonian, presented in Box 3.2.

Box 3.2 Policy innovation in outreaching rural NEETs: example from Estonia

> In Estonia, various measures have been developed for the purpose of more effectively outreaching rural NEETs. One of them is the Youth Guarantee Support System (YGSS). Through cross-sectoral cooperation involving social work, youth work, education, and internal security, among other stakeholders, this system significantly improves identification and outreach to NEETs by local authorities, thus increasing these young people's odds of returning to education, including through non-formal learning possibilities. YGSS is part of the Estonian Youth Guarantee Action Plan and is a hands-on tool for local municipalities. YGSS makes use of IT solutions for aggregating data from nine national registers in order to identify potential 16- to 26-year-old NEETs while offering case management guides for contacting target groups and offering suitable help. The long-term aim of this initiative is to support youth to go back to education or the labor market. The impact and effectiveness analysis of the implementation of the Youth Guarantee Support System points out that active labor market measures, networking, personal counseling, and prevention play a major role in supporting the continuation of young people in education and the transition to the labor market. The YGSS, in coordination with other services, directly supports the alleviation of the situation of young people in the NEET status in Estonia (Paabort, 2023).

In summary, relevant policy changes at the macrosystem involve giving priority to the education of rural NEETs. Promoting policies at the macrosystem level will generate an innovation pipeline of new tools and curricula for educators and trainers which will end up being more effective in the provision of a tailored and equitable educational system that embraces the lived experiences of rural NEETs. The bioecological model provides a useful framework for understanding the macro-level problems of rural NEETs and for identifying their needs. Policymakers, educators, and all stakeholders in education can advocate for the creation of an environment needed to shape the education of rural NEETs by taking into account the broader cultural, social, economic, and political systems thus creating the conditions for a more effective education system.

3.3 Supporting Meso-level Educational Interventions

According to the bioecological model, the mesosystem is associated with enduring and persistent forms of interactions occurring in the immediate environment of ecological systems (Bronfenbrenner, 1999). Such immediate environments can be (a) educational institutions represented by communities of teachers, mentors, trainers, educators, and associated stakeholders; (b) communities of classmates, friends, neighbors, and peers; or (c) families including parents and their children.

The mesosystem is where individual microsystems are interconnected and influence each other (Guy-Evans, 2020). An important feature of the bioecological model is that the environment, in addition to being fueled by dynamic interactions of ecosystems, also initiates and sustains continual development and changes that occur in the individuals themselves. This means that any mesosystem analysis should employ a holistic approach to the systems and real-life relationships of young people. Therefore, by using the bioecological model lens, emphasis is given to the links developed between different institutions that will ultimately have an impact on personal development, as well as on the environment itself and the unity of ecological systems. When the links between ecological systems are broken, certain developmental disparities occur in the form of disharmony or even crises, that can have implications at the community and/or personal levels. As an example, it can be said that the educational institution and the labor market represent an interconnected whole. When the links between school and the labor market are broken, this has negative impacts on each of the systems, as well as on the individuals themselves. Indicators of broken connections between ecosystems include ESLET, youth unemployment, or becoming and remaining in the NEET condition. When large shares of young people are in any of these conditions, this shows that the transition from education to employment is associated with certain deficits, while lacking the necessary skills activation and skills demand and supply matching, thus reflecting that the links between different elements of the mesosystem are broken. As a consequence of this, young people can easily fall into poverty, social exclusion, and personal disadvantage (Bronfenbrenner, 1999; Bronfenbrenner & Evans, 2000).

In countries such as Albania and Latvia, the existing indicators show some signs of a difficult connection between schools and the labor market. In 2021, the rate of young people aged 18–24 years who are early school leavers in Albania reached 17.4% while youth unemployment for those in the group 15–29 reached 20.6% (INSTAT, 2021). Overall, the labor market in Albania is characterized by decreasing but still high unemployment (12.5%), informality, low participation of youth (45.2% overall) as well as low participation of women (gender gap of 15%). Moreover, the share of NEETs in the country is above 27%. In Latvia, 9.8% of 18- to 24-year-olds had not completed school (Cabinet of Ministers Republic of Latvia, 2021), and ESLET rates are larger in rural areas. Moreover, in 2018 in Latvia, 6.2% of students in cities left school before secondary education completion compared to 13.4% of students doing the same in rural areas (Cabinet of Ministers Republic of Latvia, 2021).

Based on this data, which clearly shows disparities between rural and urban areas, particularly in Latvia, the bioecological model implies provides the opportunity for rethinking support and assistance services to young people who experience various deficits in their more localized, ecological systems. Such interventions often relate to the VET system, as well as individualized measures aimed at overcoming ESLET. Individualized measures to improve skills, as well as preparing individual plans for working with learners at risk of dropping out, represent forms of social support at the mesosystem level of intervention. Below in Box 3.3, we describe the case of Albania as a relevant example of how reforms of the VET system at the mesosystem level may come to support rural NEETs educational prospects.

Box 3.3 Reform of the VET system: example from Albania

> The reform of the VET system for improving the employment future prospects of youth is a priority of the Albanian Government. Reforms aimed at increasing the quality of education, developing adequate qualifications, fostering skills recognition, and improving the attractiveness and relevance of the VET system to match the skills demand of the private sector. To support this work the relevant macro-level policy framework is currently being improved which will, in turn, facilitate a restructuring of the governance of the sector. While this is a good example of where connections between the macro and meso-level initiatives can flourish, more efforts are needed specifically in relation to training and acquisition of professional skills and transferable skills by young people in the form of target interventions at the mesosystem level. In Albania, ongoing efforts include a movement to improve vocational education and to ensure system changes, capacity development, and empowerment of key actors in the project 'Skills for Jobs' (S4J) (INSTAT, 2021). These efforts are expected to provide young people in Albania with better vocational education and training. The project facilitates the development of quality VET offers by supporting VET providers in offering labor market integration facilities underpinned by strong networks with employers that include dual approaches and new ways of learning The outcome of this ongoing work is that young people have the opportunity to access market-oriented formal and non-formal education and training programs delivered in new and relevant ways of inclusive learning in the tourism, hospitality, construction, textile, and ICT sectors. The expected key result of the project is to improve the VSD training offer for up to 9500 young Albanian women and men and to actively place 60% among them in attractive and sustainable employment. Special consideration is given to the training and employment opportunities for young women and special-needs groups (Tase, 2023).

In Box 3.4 we also depict one example coming out from Latvia on how to shape mesosystem preventive educational interventions with a potentially positive impact on rural NEETs secondary education completion.

Box 3.4 ESLET prevention: example from Latvia

> In Latvia, one of the approaches to tackle problems faced by NEETs has been to focus on the prevention of ESLET. This goal can be effectively achieved when a strong collaboration between schools and other stakeholders is established. The support program "Pumpurs" in Latvia (European Social Fund; project Nr. 8.3.4.0/16/I/001) is mainly aimed at reducing ESLET across all key stages of secondary education (Project Pumpurs, 2022; The State Education Quality Service, 2020). It is a macrosystem level initiative that is implemented at the mesosystem level by any school and local municipality that want to become a project partner. The program is expected to involve all regions of Latvia, including rural ones. "Pumpurs" is aimed at pupils from the 1st to the 12th grade including those enrolled in VET. Students identified as those at risk can also apply individually, allowing program teams to tailor the intervention according to young people's features, thus promoting the most effective use of resources available. At the beginning of the semester, the teacher develops an individual support plan for each student involved in the program, assessing the risk of dropout. This report also outlines the necessary support measures to reduce dropout risk based on an available list of resources and activities. The outcomes of the project are divided into long and short-term outcomes. First, through the involvement of local governments and schools, individual support is provided to learners who may drop out of school due to a lack of financial resources. Expenses for transport, meals, accommodation, etc. are therefore reimbursed. However, the main focus of the project is not the provision of short-term financial assistance. Therefore, an important goal at the mesosystem level is the creation of a sustainable comprehensive mechanism that facilitates a supportive and inclusive environment for all learners. The project initially planned to involve at least 80% of local governments, covering not less than 665 general and vocational education institutions in Latvia. In 2020/2021 a total of 19,757 individual assistance and development plans were prepared as a part of the project. Funding will continue to be rolled out until 2023 (Hačatrjana, 2023).

In summary, in Albania and Latvia, the outlined projects aim to improve the VET system, providing expertise and good practices, as well as reducing early school leavers rates. They are thus fuelled by macro-level support policies for developing meso-level programs. These projects show the importance of improving links between educational institutions, the VET system, and the labor market. This interconnectedness strengthens the skills system and translates into more sustainable VET provision in the long term, preventing broken links between formal education and the work market.

3.4 Supporting Micro-level Educational Interventions

The microsystem is the level of the bioecological model comprising individuals' direct interactions in their immediate living environment, including significant others such as parents, teachers, or school peers (Bronfenbrener, 1999). Relationships at the microsystem level are bi-directional, meaning other people can influence the individuals in their environment and can also change their beliefs and actions. The interactions within microsystems are often very personal and are crucial for fostering and supporting individual development (Guy-Evans, 2020). More specifically, they are defined as a pattern of activities, social roles, and interpersonal relationships experienced by the developing person in a given face-to-face setting with particular physical, social, and symbolic features that invite, permit, or inhibit engagement in sustained, progressively more complex interaction with, and activity in, the immediate environment (Bronfenbrenner & Evans, 2000). In the literature, there are several studies underlining the key role that the microsystem plays in enhancing young people's development. The bioecological model provides the most comprehensive theoretical construct to date for investigating such interactions at the microsystem level namely in an institutional setting such as an educational one (Allen et al., 2012). According to Krishnan (2010), in the school ecological system (microsystem), as well as in non-formal education contexts, an array of direct and indirect interactions take place. Young people exist in this system of interconnected relationships, roles, activities, and settings (Shelton, 2019). This includes face-to-face interactions between students and students and students and teachers or between students and staff (Dehuff, 2013; Goodenow, 1993). Moreover, the interactions between parents and students at home, another element of the microsystem, can also increase e students' motivation and sense of belonging to their school (Uslu & Gizir, 2017).

From the bioecological perspective, a good example of the importance and impact of close networking for rural young people's school engagement at the microsystem level is the Chances program conducted in Portugal (Rodrigues, 2023). This program is part of multiple initiatives taken in the country following a major policy decision in 2009 to increase compulsory education from 9 to 12 school years (Simões et al., 2020). These initiatives have proven to be effective, according to some of the main indicators depicting young people's situation regarding school and the transition to the labour market. However, disparities remain between urban and rural areas according to different indicators. In 2022, ESLET rates in Portugal reached 6% overall but were higher in rural areas (7.9%) when compared to cities (4.4%). Seemingly, in the same year, the NEET rate for the whole country reached 8.4%. Again the share of NEETs was higher in the Portuguese countryside (9.7%) compared to Portuguese cities (7.6%). Moreover, in 2022, tertiary education attainment reached 43% in Portugal. Nevertheless, figures for this indicator were almost twice higher in Portuguese cities (47.7%) compared to rural areas (24%) across the country.

As mentioned above, the Choices program is among several on-the-ground initiatives to tackle school drop-out rates and raise school attainment levels. Choices is a nationwide government program created in 2001, whose mission is to promote social inclusion of children and young people between the ages of 6 and 25 from vulnerable socioeconomic contexts aiming at equal opportunities and strengthening social cohesion (Council of Ministers Resolution No. 71/2020). The program is project-based and the implementation of each initiative under the program is made possible through local partnerships. A specific practice of the Choices Project in a rural area of the northeast interior of Portugal aimed at promoting school success and social inclusion of children and young people, as presented below in Box 3.5.

Box 3.5 Promoting school attainment in rural areas: example from Portugal

> A study support practice was created in 2013 targeting children and young people from the neighborhoods of the intervention area of the Choices Project. The students included in the project come, in general, from families with low levels of educational attainment. Children's parents often perform unqualified jobs or are unemployed. The primary aim of the program is to foster school success and progress in school results by providing educational support centered on school guidance and follow-up providing support in individual learning and enhancing children and young people's collaborative work skills. The activities of the program are channeled towards the stimulation of cognitive and academic skills based on negotiation processes that develop from the close relationship between children and youth and the technical team fostering individualized learning (Rodrigues, 2023). These types of practices also intend to contribute to overcoming school failure, dropout, and ESLET thus focusing on individual learning, reorganization of human resources in support of learning and communication as well as collaboration among the actors involved (Antunes, 2017).
>
> The close relationship between the technical team, as significant adults, and the children and young people participating in the program has a very significant impact on the success of the activities carried out and, therefore, on school success. In general, it appears that the program enhances the capacity to generate change in both individuals and the community, constituting for most participants the only community-based response to support overcoming school failure, dropout, and ESLET and, thus, promoting social inclusion (Rodrigues, 2023).

Overall, specific interventions at the microsystem level have a crucial role in the NEET's life, in their social inclusion, and in a smoother transition to the labor market. Furthermore, this intervention shows how different educational methods can support young people and their performance. The Bioecological Model provides a useful framework for understanding the micro-level problems of rural NEETs and how such interventions like Choice can affect them at a more nuanced—personal level.

3.5 Conclusion

This chapter on education and non-formal learning presented five case studies, two at the macrosystem level, two at the mesosystem level, and one at the microsystem level of interventions. The selected interventions outlined here are primarily related to rural NEETs envisioning the long-term goals of reengaging with education, highlighting its importance for young people, or preventing ESLET through the approach. Macrosystem level interventions focused primarily on national reforms that either affect the education sector or youth support systems functioning across the country. In Estonia, for instance, various measures have been developed and one of them is the YGSS, an overall framework that has significantly improved the outreach and identification of NEETs in municipalities and better integrate them through cross-sectoral collaboration (social work, youth work, education, internal security, etc.). In Italy, we described how Law 107 was implemented in 2015 to make high secondary school less theoretical and disconnected from the labor of work, by integrating the school pathway of students with more knowledge and experience of career practices.

Both of the meso-level interventions provide insights into on-the-ground interventions. We saw that the Albanian Government is reforming the VET system and targeting the unemployment situation so that young women and men from all social groups in Albania have the opportunity to find attractive and rewarding jobs thanks to improved skills. In Latvia, there is a focus on reducing early school leaving and it is organized as a national-level program where an individualized approach to educational engagement is central to activities. An additional example from Portugal illustrates interventions conducted at the microsystem level, highlighting the role of non-formal education in addressing regional inequality and establishing a positive influence on youth performances ahead of entering the labor market.

It is clear that formal education and non-formal learning intervention or reforms, at all levels, have an important function in the NEET or at-risk youth support system. Interventions or reforms that support the development of young people or prevent them from falling into the NEET status are critically important. However, they can only be effective when designed to respond to the contextual sensitivities of the young people that they target. The bioecological model provides us with a framework for improving contextual sensitivity of educational policies and interventions work and for understanding the complex relationship between opportunities for rural NEET young people and different policies and programs operating at various levels.

3.5.1 New Research Developments

Based on the work presented in this chapter, we consider that the following areas should frame new research developments.

- **A comprehensive review of educational policy that targets rural youth.** It is clear from the development of this chapter that more work is needed to develop a clear understanding of the European educational policy landscape cognizant of the jurisdictional sensitivities of state-level ministries of education. This work is essential for enabling an effective sharing of best practices.
- **A structured program of research to develop a deeper understanding of the horizontal traits of effective interventions.** While the work presented here provides critical insight into educational programs that are making a difference for rural young people it is also clear that we do not know enough about how such programs generate impacts in the short, medium, and long term, beyond large-scale data sets.
- **The development of a dedicated dissemination pathway for sharing best practices.** In order to share best practices it is essential that the research ecosystem that has emerged from the COST Action Rural NEET Youth Network develops a long-term, sustainable ecosystem so that the aforementioned recommendations can be actioned.

3.5.2 Policy Recommendations

- Based on the work presented in this chapter, the following general recommendations can be made for policy development.
- **Macrosystem level policy decisions need to be informed by meso and micro-level research.** While large-scale datasets provide direction, it is clear that the rich, qualitative smaller-scale studies could provide policymakers with critical markers of success.
- **Mesosystem level actors can act as connectors between the various levels.** State or regional-level decision-makers and intervention designers are ideally placed to develop an environment where conversations between policymakers and those who carry out work on the ground can engage in a dialogue focused on educational design that seeks to target rural youth.
- **Successful microsystem level interventions should be modeled for replication.** Currently, micro-level interventions are rarely modeled for replication. They are generally highlighted as successful. Given the work in this chapter, which has highlighted that local sensitivity and contextualization are key characteristics of any successful intervention, it is vital that those who may seek to replicate such work understand the 'how' of that action.

References

Allen, A. (2012). Understanding environmental change in the context of rural–urban interactions. In *The Peri-Urban interface* (pp. 53–66). Routledge.

Antunes, F. (2017). Locais Educadores: Práticas, vozes e percursos de educação inclusiva (EDUPLACES). *Jornal de Sociologia da Educação, 1*, 1–9.

Bronfenbrenner, U. (1999). Environments in developmental perspective: Theoretical and operational models. In S. L. Friedman & T. D. Wachs (Eds.), *Measuring environment across the life span: Emerging methods and concepts* (pp. 3–28). American Psychological Association Press. https://doi.org/10.1037/10317-001

Bronfenbrenner, U., & Evans, G. W. (2000). Developmental science in the 21st century: Emerging questions, theoretical models, research designs and empirical findings. *Social Development, 9*(1), 115–125. https://doi.org/10.1111/1467-9507.00114

Cabinet of Ministers of the Republic of Latvia. (2021). *Izglītības attīstības pamatnostādnes 2021.-2027.gadam*. [Guidelines for the development of education for 2021-2027, Rules Nr.436]. Accessed June 3, 2022, from www.likumi.lv

Council of Ministers. (2020). *Resolution of the Council of Ministers No. 71/2020 of 15 September (approves the renewal of the Choices Programme for the period 2021-2022)*.

Dehuff, P. A. (2013). *Students' wellbeing and sense of belonging: A qualitative study of relationship and interactions in a small school district* [Doctoral dissertation]. Available from ProQuest Dissertations & Theses database (UMI No. 3587070).

Erdoğan, E., Uyan, P., & Petrescu, C. (2022). *Manual for the methodological best-practices in research dedicated to rural NEETs*. ISBN: 978-989-781-613-0.

Eurostat. (2020). *Young people neither in employment nor in education and training by sex, age and labour status (NEET rates)*. https://ec.europa.eu/eurostat.

Goodenow, C. (1993). Classroom belonging among early adolescent students' relationships to motivation and achievement. *The Journal of Early Adolescence, 13*, 21–43. https://doi.org/10.1177/0272431693013001002

Guy-Evans, O. (2020). *Bronfenbrenner's ecological systems theory*. Simply Psychology. Accessed February 21, 2023, from www.simplypsychology.org/Bronfenbrenner.html

Hačatrjana, L. (2023). *A National level Intervention Program "Pumpurs" in Latvia for prevention of leaving school for youth at risk: Involving schools, municipalities, teachers, students and NGOs*. Best practice interventions in Formal and Non-formal Education of Youth NEETs in Rural Areas Across Europe. ISBN: 978-989-781-757-1.

INSTAT. (2021). *Albania*.

Krishnan, V. (2010). *Early child development: A conceptual model* [Paper presentation]. Early childhood Council Annual Conference, "Valuing Care," Christchurch Convention Center, Christchurch, New Zealand.

Paabort, H. (2023). *Estonian Youth Guarantee Support System*. Best practice interventions in Formal and Non-formal Education of Youth NEETs in Rural Areas Across Europe. ISBN: 978-989-781-757-1

Petrescu, C., Pilařová, T., Paabort, H., Nasya, B., Marta, E., Fernandes-Jesus, M., Bojnec, S., Erdoğan, E., Flynn, P., & Soler, M. (2020). *Manual for the classification of intervention best-practices with rural NEETs*. https://doi.org/10.15847/CISRNYN.MN1.2020.12

Project Pumpurs. (2022). *Project "Pumpurs" web page*. Accessed May 10, 2022, from www.pumpurs.lv

Rocca, A. (2023). *The school-work alternation*. Best practice interventions in Formal and Non-formal Education of Youth NEETs in Rural Areas Across Europe. ISBN: 978-989-781-757-1.

Rodrigues, M. O. (2023). *Promoting academic success and social inclusion in non-formal education contexts in a northeast region of Portugal*. Best practice interventions in Formal and Non-formal Education of Youth NEETs in Rural Areas Across Europe. ISBN: 978-989-781-757-1.

Shelton, L. G. (2019). *The Bronfenbrenner primer: A guide to Develecology*. Routledge.

Simões, F., Tosun, J., & Rocca, A. (2022). Determinants of job-finding intentions among young adults from 11 European countries. *Social Indicators Research, 164*(2), 623–648. https://doi.org/10.1007/s11205-022-02941-6

Simões, F. (2023). Equal opportunities, fair work and social protection: Impacts of COVID-19 on young people in Portuguese rural territories. In E. Medeiros (Ed.), *Public policies for territorial cohesion*. Springer.

Simões, F., Ferreira, T., & Vieira, M. M. (2020). *COST CA18213 Rural NEETs in Portugal: 2009/ 2019 overview*.

Tase, M. (2023). *Skills for jobs, vocational training employment & economic development in Albania (first phase), vocational training advanced professional training SME development (second phase)*. Best practice interventions in Formal and Non-formal Education of Youth NEETs in Rural Areas Across Europe. ISBN: 978-989-781-757-1.

Tatiana, F., Ellena, A. M., Maria, F. J., Frida, J., Belém, B., Emelj, T., et al. (2023). *Mapping community-based projects promoting participation and social inclusion of youth NEETs in rural areas across Europe*.

The State Education Quality Service. (2020). *Eiropas Sociālā fonda projekta Nr.8.3.4.0/16/I/001 "Atbalsts priekšlaicīgas mācību pārtraukšanas samazināšanai" ietekmes pušu iesaistes, informētības un starprezultātu novērtējuma pētījums* [European Social Fund project no. 8.3.4.0/16/I/001 "Support to reduce early school leaving" stakeholder engagement, awareness and interim results evaluation study]. Accessed October 10, 2022, from http://www.pumpurs.lv/sites/default/files/2020-06/IKVD_Pumpurs_Petijums_GALA_ZINOJUMS_29_0 6_2020.pdf

Uslu, F., & Gizir, S. (2017). School belonging of adolescents: The role of teacher-student relationships, peer relationships, and family involvement. *Educational Sciences: Theory & Practice, 17*(1), 63. https://doi.org/10.12738/estp.2017.1.0104

Open Access This chapter is licensed under the terms of the Creative Commons Attribution 4.0 International License (http://creativecommons.org/licenses/by/4.0/), which permits use, sharing, adaptation, distribution and reproduction in any medium or format, as long as you give appropriate credit to the original author(s) and the source, provide a link to the Creative Commons license and indicate if changes were made.

The images or other third party material in this chapter are included in the chapter's Creative Commons license, unless indicated otherwise in a credit line to the material. If material is not included in the chapter's Creative Commons license and your intended use is not permitted by statutory regulation or exceeds the permitted use, you will need to obtain permission directly from the copyright holder.

Chapter 4
Rural Dimension of the Employment Policies for NEETs. A Comparative Analysis of the Reinforced Youth Guarantee

Claudia Petrescu, Ruta Braziene, Òscar Prieto-Flores, Mariano Soler, Anastasia Costantini, Bianca Buligescu, Daiva Skuciene, Antonella Rocca, Federica Pizzolante, Luca Koltai, Mateusz Smoter, and Sylwia Danilowska

Abstract In 2020, the European Commission relaunched the Youth Guarantee (YG) Programme, its flagship policy for youth unemployment since 2013. This action aims to renew the European Union efforts on promoting the employment of those below 30 years old in the aftermath of the COVID-19 pandemic. All EU member states adapted this EU directive to their national policies releasing their own national strategies. One of the novelties of this transnational policy initiative is its emphasis on targeting youth living in rural, remote, or disadvantaged areas. This book chapter analyzes how different EU countries are adapting this policy at the national level and how they integrate the rural dimension in the proposed measures.

C. Petrescu (✉) · B. Buligescu
Research Institute for Quality of Life, Romanian Academy, Bucharest, Romania
e-mail: claudia.petrescu@iccv.ro

R. Braziene · D. Skuciene
Vilnius University, Vilnius, Lithuania

Ò. Prieto-Flores
University of Girona, Girona, Spain

M. Soler
Universidad de Málaga, Málaga, Spain

A. Costantini
Diesis Network, Brussels, Belgium

A. Rocca · F. Pizzolante
Parthenope University of Naples, Naples, Italy

L. Koltai
Hétfa Research Institute, Budapest, Hungary

M. Smoter
Institute for Structural Research, Wrocław, Poland

S. Danilowska
Activation Foundation, Wrocław, Poland

© The Author(s) 2024
F. Simões, E. Erdogan (eds.), *NEETs in European rural areas*, SpringerBriefs in Sociology, https://doi.org/10.1007/978-3-031-45679-4_4

Commonalities and differences in approaches and types of actions to be implemented across countries will be discussed.

Keywords NEETs · Policies · Youth Guarantee · (Un)employment · Disadvantaged areas

4.1 Introduction

A new EU Youth Strategy was adopted in 2018 setting out a framework for cooperation with Member States on their youth policies for the 2019–2027 period. The strategy focuses on three core areas of action, centered around the words 'engage, connect, empower'. The COVID-19 pandemic had a serious impact on the implementation of apprenticeships and training as well as on youth employment according to the study developed by Eurofound (2021) on this topic. To support the economic recovery from the pandemic, on the 1st of July 2020, the European Commission launched a Youth Employment Support package (European Commission, 2020b) to further support youth employment for the next generation. More specifically, the European Commission put forward a proposal for a Council Recommendation on 'A Bridge to Jobs—Reinforcing the Youth Guarantee', to improve the 2013 Recommendation, introducing new measures that facilitate the green and digital transition for young people, and fostering vocational education and training and apprenticeship. In addition, the European Pillar of Social Rights Action Plan, proposed by the European Commission in March 2021 and followed by a declaration at the Porto Social Summit in May 2021, introduced new, ambitious targets for young people, such as reducing the rate of young people Not in Employment, nor in Education or Training (NEET) from 12.6% (2019) to 9% by 2030.

The relaunch of the Youth Guarantee (YG) Programme as a reinforced program by the European Commission is an initiative that aims to renew the efforts on promoting the employment of those below 30 years old in the aftermath of COVID-19. The Reinforced Youth Guarantee (RYG) scheme provides EU Member States the opportunity for all young people under 30 years of age to access employment, education, apprenticeship, or traineeship within 4 months of either leaving education or becoming newly unemployed. This framework was reinforced for better responding to younger generations' needs during the pandemic period. The RYG is aiming at dealing with the COVID-19 pandemic's effects on European youth unemployment and social inclusion and to prevent another youth employment crisis. The renewed supportive mechanism has broadened the target group, currently including young people from 15- to 29-year-olds. The predominant operative ambition is to set up solid national schemes in which young people can have direct and straightforward access to work, education, or training offers (European Commission, 2020b).

COVID-19 EU PolicyWatch (Eurofound, 2020), an initiative developed by the Eurofound to map policy measures introduced in the EU member states to cushion the social and economic effects of the latest sanitary crisis pandemic on businesses, workers and citizens, organized a database for describing the responses of governments and social partners to the COVID-19 crisis. Despite the fact that there were more than 2700 different measures proposed since 2020 (income support, direct subsidies, active labor market measures, working conditions protection, etc.), young people were not always covered by the social protection measures.

Young people's situation in the labor market is particularly affected by socioeconomic crises. The 2008 financial crisis and the current crisis caused by the COVID-19 pandemic has a negative impact on youth employment levels and young people's working conditions, job search, and employability, making them an even more vulnerable group in the labor market (ILO, 2021; Eurofound, 2021; OECD, 2021; European Commission, 2020a). Youth joblessness has been a recurring consequence of recessions, as young people have lower levels of job security and are at greater risk of job loss. In particular, the COVID-19 crisis hit socially vulnerable groups of young people (NEET youth, unemployed young people, or young people in non-standard employment such as temporary workers, workers in atypical employment, etc.) (Eurofound, 2021; ILO, 2021, 2022; McKinsey, 2020; Simões, 2022). Indeed, due to the COVID-19 pandemic, youth employment declined in many European countries. The analysis of labor market statistics and surveys indicates a significantly larger rate of job loss among young people than among people aged 30 or over (Eurofound, 2021). The major job losses are in sectors that employ a large proportion of young people with insecure contracts (Eurofound, 2021).

As RYG's measures should be transposed at the national level, it represents a good starting point to understand the objectives of the national policies in the youth employment area, but also of the integrated approach followed by each country to tackle the NEETs issues. By the end of 2021, some countries had presented RYG implementation plans (e.g. Lithuania,[1] Italy, Poland,[2] Spain[3]) or had introduced measures related to RYG in the national strategies for employment (e.g. Romania[4]). As not all countries had implemented the RYG plans until June 2023 (e.g. Hungary), it is difficult to have a clear picture of the proposed measures and how the programme have been transposed and adapted from the EU level to the national/local contexts.

Despite all these constraints, our chapter aims to offer a better understanding of the measures dedicated to youth from rural or other disadvantaged areas within RYG. Specifically, this chapter aims to identify how different EU countries are adapting the Reinforced Youth Guarantee in their national contexts and how they

---

[1] Action Plan for the Implementation of the Youth Guarantee Initiative in Lituania (2021). https://e-seimas.lrs.lt/portal/legalAct/lt/TAD/7a882e72672811eb9954cfa9b9131808

[2] Youth Guarantee Implementation Plan in Poland, Ministerstwo Pracy i Polityki Społecznej (praca.gov.pl)

[3] Servicio Publico de Empleo Estatal (2021). Youth Guarantee. Retrieved from https://www.sepe.es/HomeSepe/que-es-el-sepe/comunicacion-institucional/noticias/detalle-noticia.html?folder=/2021/Junio/&detail=Plan-de-Garantia-Juvenil-Plus-2021-2027

[4] Romania. Ministry of Labour and Social Protection (2021). The national Strategy for Employment 2021–2027. https://mmuncii.ro/j33/images/Documente/MMPS/SNOFM_2021-2027.pdf

integrate this rural dimension in the proposed measures. Commonalities and differences in approaches and types of actions to be implemented across countries will be analyzed.

4.2 Conceptual Framework

This chapter draws on Bronfenbrenner's bioecological model of personal development (Bronfenbrenner, 1979; Bronfenbrenner & Evans, 2000). Specifically, our work focuses on analyzing the general policy framework that has a significant impact on youth employment at the EU level. The bioecological model highlights the prominent role that contextual factors at different levels play in mediating an individual's specific developmental pathway (Lőrinc et al., 2020). The RYG policy framework is, thus, part of the macrosystem of the bioecological model, constituted by structural conditions and political factors of young rural NEETs integration in school, apprenticeship, or employment pathways.

According to the Bronfenbrenner's bioecological theory (Bronfenbrenner & Evans, 2000), young adults' transitions to adulthood and integration in the labor market are influenced by multiple systems, including the microsystem (e.g., family poverty level, school infrastructure problems, peers influence), mesosystem (e.g., home-school partnership), exosystem (e.g., community type, extended family, neighborhood, media, social services, local politics, local labor market), and macrosystem (e.g., rural culture, education system, public policy, attitudes and values, laws, political system, economic system) (Iruka et al., 2020; Lőrinc et al., 2020).

Our analysis aims to identify how the public policy framework addresses the transition to the labor market and what measures tackle rural youth issues in six EU countries (Hungary, Italy, Lithuania, Poland, Romania, and Spain). Moreover, this chapter is based on the results of the report *Employment and Employment Services for Rural NEETs: Initiatives for Tackling NEETs' and Rural NEETs' Employment Issues* (Petrescu & Prieto-Flores, 2023) and the policy report *Youth employment Support Services and Advancing Green Job Opportunities* (Petrescu & Costantini, 2023) developed within the Work Group 3 Employment Services and Employment in Rural areas of the COST Action Rural NEET Youth Network.

4.3 Characteristics of Youth Living in Rural, Remote, or Disadvantaged Areas in Hungary, Italy, Lithuania, Poland, Romania, and Spain

In many countries, rural young people who are in the NEET condition face problems associated with social exclusion, lack of opportunities (e.g. education, health, infrastructure, public transport, labor market conditions) or low socio-economic status.

The most common risk factors affecting this group of vulnerable young people include socio-economically disadvantaged environments, low level of education and school problems, lack of adequate housing, financial problems, learning difficulties, dissatisfaction with school; socio-emotional disorders, delinquency, health problems, homelessness, and drug or alcohol abuse (Mauro Ellena et al., 2021; Petrescu et al., 2022; Simões et al., 2017; Sadler et al., 2015). Sparsely populated, rural areas have the highest rates of NEETs, while densely populated, urban areas—where there are typically more jobs, better physical infrastructure and quality of public transport, and higher average educational attainment—have the lowest (Eurostat, 2023; Mukherjee, 2012; Petrescu et al., 2022; Simões et al., 2017; Sadler et al., 2015).

The annual Eurostat report about young people aged 15–29 in the NEET condition (Eurostat, 2023) indicates that there are considerable differences between NEET rates in urban areas (cities), towns and suburbs, and rural areas. The Eurostat data on NEETs by the degree of urbanization during the last decade (2013–2021) indicates that the share of this group of young people in rural areas is larger than in urban areas in many countries (Romania, Bulgaria, Hungary, Lithuania, Letonia, Poland, etc.) by 10%, 15% or 20% and well above the EU-27 average level. The average results for EU-27 countries show the lowest NEET rate occurs in cities, slightly higher in towns and suburbs, while in rural areas the rate is the highest in the above-mentioned countries. The most unfavorable position of young adults from rural areas is observed in Italy and Romania. Italy is one of the countries with the lowest differences among rural/urban areas. Poland is among the countries where the NEET rate in the group of people aged 15–29 is close to the EU average. In 2021, it amounted to 13.4% in Poland compared to 13.1% in the EU27. Rural areas and towns displayed higher NEET rates than cities across all age subgroups. The difference is especially visible in the 25–29 age group, in which the NEET rate gap between cities and rural areas reached almost 11 pp (11.1% in cities vs. 21.8% in rural areas). The gap has been quite stable for over a decade, which means that rural areas and small towns did not converge with cities. The COVID-19-related growth of the NEET rate is more visible in rural areas (Romania, Hungary, Spain, Lithuania) as well as in towns and suburbs (Spain) than in cities (see Fig. 4.1).

Rural NEETs face several barriers that have been mentioned before (limited access to labor market due to lack of transport opportunities, low education level, lack of information and employment opportunities) making it difficult for them to enter the job market or pursue education and training (Petrescu et al., 2022; Sadler et al., 2015; Simões et al., 2017). Young people in rural areas usually have lower levels of education compared to their urban counterparts. This can make it more challenging for them to find employment, particularly in fields that require specialized knowledge or training.

Education is very important for youth integration into the labor market being one of the trigger factors for becoming NEET. Leaving education early can also have significant consequences for the individual, as well as for society, in the long term such as an increased risk of poverty and social exclusion, poverty in work due to low-paid jobs, low self-esteem, mental health issues, alcohol and drug abuse etc.

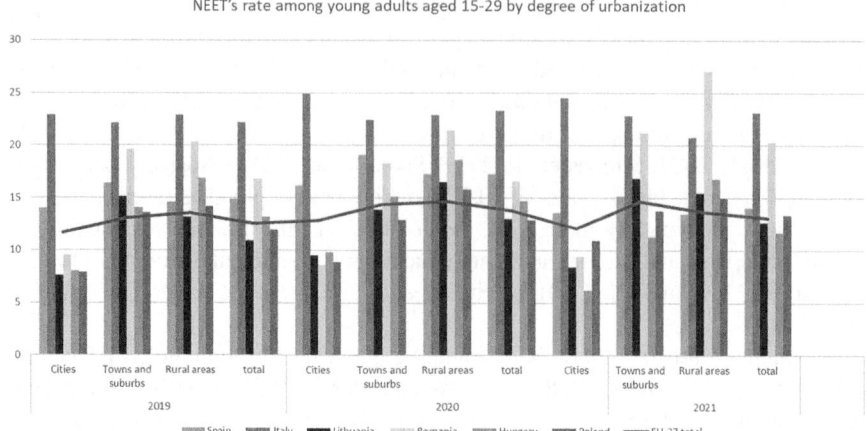

Fig. 4.1 NEET's rate among young adults aged 15–29 by degree of urbanization, 2019–2021 (%). Source: Eurostat—Labour Force Survey [EDAT_LFSE_29]; data extraction on 27.05.23

(Burlina et al., 2021; EUROFOUND, 2016; Lawy et al., 2010; De Luca et al., 2020; Madia et al., 2022; Smoter, 2022). The European Union Council set a target that the share of early leavers from education and training should be less than 9% by 2030 (Council of the European Union, 2021). In 2022, an average of 9.6% of early leavers from education and training was identified within the EU and the early school leaving rate differs considerably in selected countries. Among the countries included in our analyses, the highest early school leaving rates in rural areas are observed in Romania (24.5%) and Hungary (19.7%) (see Fig. 4.2).

4.4 The Reinforced Youth Guarantee Programme in Hungary, Italy, Spain, Romania, Poland, and Lithuania and the Integration of Rural, Remote or Disadvantaged Areas Dimension

The YG scheme is the EU flagship initiative launched in 2013 targeting the transition of NEET youth to employment, education or training. To monitor the progress of YG at the national level, each country delivers yearly fiches [5] providing information about the implementation of the program at the national level. As for EU27, the coverage of NEETs by the YG is 40.3% in 2020, but this percentage differs considerably among countries. In the countries analyzed in this chapter, the highest YG coverage is observed in Lithuania (65.9%) and Poland (42.8%) and the lowest

---

[5] https://ec.europa.eu/social/main.jsp?advSearchKey=YGYEI&mode=advancedSubmit&catId=1307&doc_submit=&policyArea=0&policyAreaSub=0&country=0&year=0

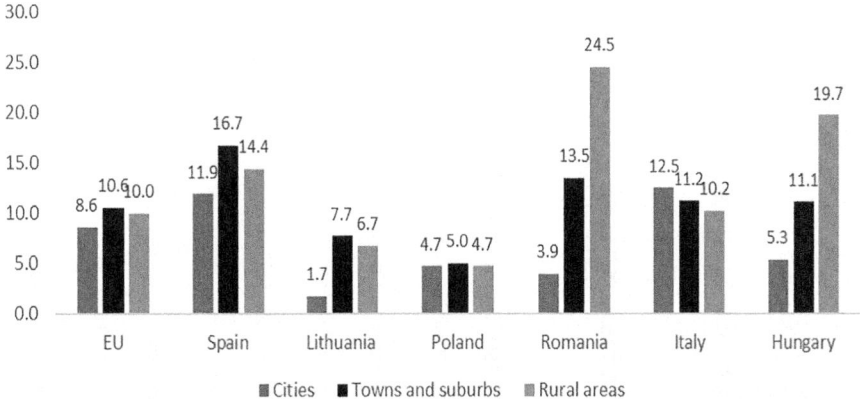

Fig. 4.2 Early leavers from education and training by degree of urbanization, 2022 (% of population aged 18–24). Source: Eurostat—Labour Force Survey [EDAT_LFSE_30]; data extraction on 23.04.2023

coverage is reported for Hungary (2.6%), Italy (11.2%), and Romania (8.9%). The take-up of a training, apprenticeship, or employment offer within 4 months also differs by country. The highest take-up offer is in Hungary (89.9%) and the lowest in Spain (9.1%) in 2020 (see Fig. 4.3).

Considering the success of the YG measures in EU countries and following the COVID-19 pandemic impact on youth employment, the European Commission relaunched the RYG aiming to create employment opportunities for young people or to increase the space for employment opportunities by improving skills and competences, including upskilling and reskilling. In the context of the twin transition (digital and green), RYG includes measures to learn or improve digital and green competencies and skills of young people. Each country from our analysis included these measures in their RYG national plans/strategies (approved or in the process to be approved like in Hungary) for learning or improving digital and green competencies as mandatory for young people covered by the policy.

The most important active labor market instruments considered in the RYG at the EU and national levels are apprenticeships and traineeships, given the previous results achieved through their implementation (Broeck et al., 2017). These are considered by the RYG in the analyzed countries as important policy instruments both for facilitating the transition of young people to the labor market and for involving the business sector in this process of increasing youth employment by addressing their skills needs (Petrescu & Prietro-Flores, 2023).

Given the main challenges in the implementation of YG and the need to increase youth employment, the European Commission proposes a new approach to tackle youth problems that includes four stages: mapping, outreach, preparation, and offer. At the same time, RYG mainstreams the individualized and integrated approach as the best option in dealing with NEETs due to the diversity of national, regional, or local socio-economic contexts and their categories and characteristics. The one-stop-

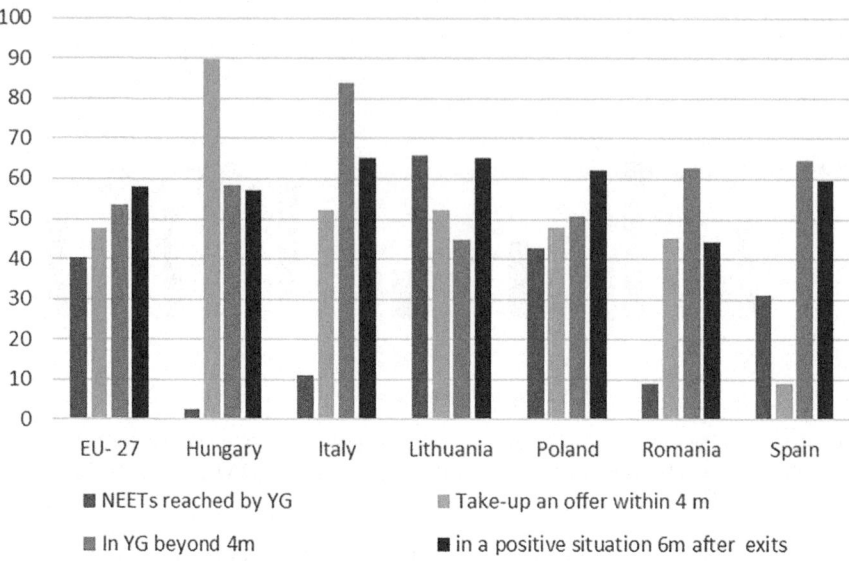

Fig. 4.3 NEET's reached by the Youth Guarantee at EU and national level (%). Source: https://ec.europa.eu/social/main.jsp?catId=1161&langId=en. Notes: (1) However, a number of countries do not report on 25–29 age group (among which Hungary), (2) For Hungary when the denominator of the coverage indicator is restricted to the 15–24 age-group, then still only a 5.3% of young NEETs are reached by the YG

shop model is promoted as one of integrated service provision for NEETs by RYG which proposes also preparatory training (with digital, green, language, entrepreneurial, and career management skills) before taking up an offer. Also, better coordination and partnership between policy areas (employment, education, youth, social and gender equality) is a condition for NEETs integration into the labor market and in society. All these measures for the EU level are transposed at the national/regional level but the national plans for implementation of RYG should be adapted to the national context and needs. In the countries covered by this chapter, these measures are included in the national plans/strategies.

The development of the RYG at national level and the specific measures for NEETs from rural, remote, or disadvantaged areas were based on a combination of empirical evidence, stakeholder consultations, and best practices from other countries and regions (Petrescu & Pietro-Flores, 2023; Petrescu & Costantini, 2023). As countries implemented several policies aimed at reducing youth unemployment in the past, the evaluations of these policies were used to inform the development of the RYG. These evaluations provided insights about the strengths and weaknesses of previous policies and identified areas where improvements were needed.

By 2021, some of the countries covered by this chapter have already presented RYG implementation plans (Lithuania, Spain, Poland) or included RYG measures in the national strategy of employment (Romania). In Hungary, the National YG Implementation Plan dated 2014 is still in place (Government of Hungary, 2014) and the original measures have been extended to a wider age group in 2022 (Bördős et al., 2022).

4.4.1 The Reinforced Youth Guarantee for Rural NEETs: A Country by Country Analysis

Like many other EU countries, **Spain** presented the first YG Implementation Plan on 19 December 2013 (European Commission, 2020b). The last program called "Youth Guarantee Plan Plus 2021–2027 for decent work for young people" was approved on 9 June 2021 with a total budget of 4.950 million euros divided into different programs (SEPE, 2021). The pillars of the Plan focus on (a) improving the employability and entrepreneurship of young people, based on personalized guidance and monitoring of users in all support actions; (b) training aimed at acquiring skills and improving the professional experience, taking into account the needs to transform the production model; (c) improving employment opportunities through targeted incentives, especially for people who need special consideration; (d) promoting equal opportunities; and (e) upholding entrepreneurship and promotion of business initiative and improvement of management (SEPE, 2021). Some of the specific measures included in this plan are flexibility and agility of management and entrepreneurship for young people affected by the health crisis, caused by the COVID-19 pandemic. This program grants microcredits for young people who cannot access ordinary credit to obtain financing, without the need for guarantees. Microcredits could be used by young people to develop a business or to continue their education. In addition, the plan promotes the reinforcement of professional career guidance. To address gender inequalities, the plan also proposes some measures for women with family responsibilities or in other vulnerable situations. The plan emphasizes the need of personalized itineraries for various categories of vulnerable young people (with disabilities, early school leavers, migrants, LGBTQI etc.).

Spain is among the countries that have presented specific measures to support NEETs from rural, remote, or disadvantaged areas ("Youth Guarantee Plan Plus 2021–2027 for decent work for young people"). Regeneration of rural and urban spaces in decline is seen as a key action to recover these environments and to open a window of opportunity to generate youth employment. The orientation for the regeneration of rural and urban spaces is a measure aimed especially at young people with creative initiative who seek to carry out actions with a social purpose. All of this will allow for a double impact: job creation and response to the housing demand of vulnerable people. The generational succession measures in rural areas are aimed at giving generational relief in traditional jobs. The enhancement of the historical, natural, and cultural heritage, the recovery of trades, and the generation of job opportunities are encouraged through the promotion of workshops, employment workshops, and mixed Employment-Training programs. The Employment-Training programs will include professional experience in companies in the intervention territories, with special attention to training and employment within the framework of rural tourism. The Redes Taller Joven program will facilitate mobility within the national territory based on the interests of young people with specific help that will improve their opportunities.

In **Lithuania**, the new action plan for the implementation of the RYG initiative was approved in 2021. The aim of the new plan is "to ensure that all persons aged 15–29 who are not in employment, education or training receive an offer to work, continue learning (including professional training in the form of an apprenticeship, practice or an internship)". During the implementation of the plan, services are provided to inactive and unemployed young persons aged 16–29. The new RYG action plan implementation proposes that most of the attention should be paid to persons with medium and limited employment opportunities, who display low motivation levels, are already long-term unemployed, or are at risk of becoming unemployed without additional help. Since the long-term unemployed are one of the most vulnerable groups in society and they are particularly at risk of becoming socially excluded, the first priority should be to prevent individuals from becoming long-term unemployed.

The Lithuanian RYG plan lacks specific measures targeting NEET young people from rural, remote, or disadvantaged areas. In comparison to the previous plan, the Reinforced Youth Guarantee initiative in Lithuania includes the provision of professional guidance services and monitoring the number of inactive young people in all its municipalities.

Italy is advancing in the implementation of the RYG scheme, which is comprehensive and based on a partnership strategy, combined with a strong profiling methodology that aims at a personalized approach and the development of successful individual pathways. Still, the Italian levels of unemployed youth and NEET rates are the highest in the EU, and large disparities across the northern and southern regions persist.

Geared to national, regional, and local circumstances, the RYG is based on building partnership-based approaches which may be less strong in rural areas. Nevertheless, the problem of rural youth is mentioned more in the public debate, but it is still not very well represented in the policy measures. As the Italian context is characterized by many small villages and rural areas, specific measures which take into account all the characteristics of these areas should be implemented.

The new RYG implementation plan in **Poland** was approved in 2022 and relies on four pillars—Public Employment Service (PES), Voluntary Labor Corps (VLC), central and regional projects, and a loan program. Based on the diagnosis of the situation of young people in the labor market, five priority groups were identified in the RYG: those aged 15–17 who dropped out of school or have neglected compulsory schooling or education; persons aged 18–29, registered as unemployed; NEET youth; people who are unemployed or looking for a job, people finishing their education or university graduates; people who have left foster care; women under 30 raising children.

As in many other countries, rural NEETs were not identified as a priority group in Polish RYG. However, within the RYG, a strong emphasis will be put on improving strategies that allow PES to reach out to individuals living in rural and remote areas. This is the main change compared to the YG plan from 2014–2020 and this will affect mainly NEETs from rural areas. The outreach activities within the RYG strategies will be based on the following (a) improved cooperation with local grassroots organisations that work with young people on a daily basis; (b) mobile information points that will provide PES services in remote areas; (c) information campaigns in local media and social media; (d) stronger cooperation with job advisors in local schools; (e) more services offered via online meeting platforms; and (f) presence of PES outreach teams in local events (sport, cultural, other local events). These activities will be carried out both by PES and VLC employees. Besides, NEETs from rural areas will be eligible to use various Active Labor Market Policies (ALMPs) and services provided by PES within the RYG. Importantly, the YG in Poland has directed EU funds to finance various projects within the RYG. In the upcoming years, the crucial measure of the Polish RYG will be the European Funds for Social Development Programme (FERS) (a new initiative dedicated to social inclusion in the European Multi-Annual Financial Framework 2021–2027). The modernization of the PES is planned in FERS (e.g., developing uniform quality standards for the functioning of PES and VLC, or ensuring effective coordination of activities aimed at young people), within the framework of the rules set out in the reinforced YG and the long-term unemployed. Professional activation covering unemployed young people and those in a difficult situation on the labor market will be implemented as well.

In **Hungary**, the RYG was transposed into a national plan but it has not been approved yet. At the same time, very little information is currently available on the spatial characteristics of YG implementation.

Overall, nearly half of those covered by the program (a slightly higher proportion of the long-term unemployed) live in more disadvantaged rural settlements or sparsely populated areas of Hungary. Looking at the drop-out rate of the target group, the Equinox (2018) impact evaluation study showed that some groups, such as women and disadvantaged people, are less likely to complete the program successfully (although the effect is not significant) and that those living in large cities have a higher drop-out rate than their rural counterparts, while higher educational attainment significantly increases the chances of successful completion. Importantly, two-thirds of participants of the apprenticeship program live in rural areas (Koping-Tárki, 2021).

In **Romania**, the RYG is part of the National Strategy of Employment 2021–2027. The measures/actions included in the National Strategy for Employment for 2021–2027 for young people are (a) the development of prevention systems by strengthening partnerships between institutions with competencies in the field of employment, education, and social protection and other entities to identify young people at risk of becoming NEET; (b) the establishment/development of youth centers/clubs at the community level; (c) mapping, informing, preparing, and providing the offer itself (integrated packages of activation measures for young people, including NEETs); (d) improving the tracking system of the situation of NEETs after integration into the labor market or into the education or training system;

(e) developing volunteering among young people, including NEETs; and (f) ensuring that young people, including NEETs, acquire transversal skills, with a focus on basic digital skills, career management, communication, and teamwork skills, as well as social and green entrepreneurship skills.

There are no specific measures for NEETs from rural areas even if the urban-rural gap is mentioned in the context analysis of the Romanian National Strategy of Employment 2021–2027. As in other countries (e.g. Poland, Bulgaria, Hungary etc), the percentage of rural NEETs is higher in Romania and also other categories of NEETs are more prevalent in the countryside (long-term unemployment, young people with disabilities, young people with family responsibilities). The National Strategy of Employment 2021–2027 recognized all these problems and NEETs different profiles in the context analysis, but their specific needs are supposed to be addressed not through dedicated policy measures, but through individualized intervention. The Romanian approach is not, therefore, to propose specific policy measures, but to provide young people with the resources after mapping their needs, because the individualized intervention should tackle all NEETs issues and be tailored to each individual. According to the Strategy objective focusing on NEETs, the integrated packages of activation measures may include counseling, mediation, subsidies, vocational training/internships/internships, skills assessment, enrolment, and support for participation in flexible second-chance programs, including vocational training modules, provision of personalized support services (training allowances to cover training-related expenses—transport, meals, etc.), subsidizing the costs of obtaining a driver's license, internship, apprenticeship, mobility allowances, employment allowances.

4.5 Conclusion

Due to the COVID 19 pandemic the overall unemployment rate increase in Europe and affected to a high extent young people (Eurofound, 2021). Pandemic related measures led rural youth to be among the groups that were more likely to lose their jobs and to have limited access to education. Despite all the challenges in implementing YG, this initiative has positively influenced the national policy framework in the field of youth employment (Petrescu et al., 2021; Petrescu et al., 2022). The RYG continues the implementation of the measures proposed by the YG and is the public policy that defines the intervention framework for increasing youth employment at EU and national level.

The European Commission intended to provide an effective response to youth unemployment through the RYG and also to introduce new perspectives and new opportunities for working with NEETs. Although the European Commission requires Member States to adapt these measures from RYG to the specificities and needs of young people at national level, the transposition of the measures into national policy is sometimes limited and there are no specific measures for certain categories of young people/NEETs or for those from rural or vulnerable areas. This is worthwhile to note given that according to official data (e.g., Eurostat) a higher number of NEETs live in rural or remote/vulnerable areas including in several of the countries covered by our analysis.

The evidence supporting the national RYGs/strategy for NEETs further justifies the proposed measures to a large extent, but there are still no specific measures for young NEETs in rural areas (although they are the most numerous). The analysis of RYG demonstrates that from all the countries analyzed Spain is the only country where there are specific measures dedicated to NEET youth from rural, remote and disadvantaged areas. In Lithuania, Spain, Romania, Poland and Italy some measures have been issued for specific categories of NEETs such as long term unemployed, young people with disabilities or those who have family responsibilities (young mothers with children, young people that take care of other family members etc.).

Rural NEETs are not defined as a priority target group within the RYG and no measures dedicated to this group have been introduced in most of the countries included in our analysis. The good side of the RYG is that the outreach activities seem to have gained priority. This is important from the rural NEETs' perspective as it may bring them closer to the public employment services. Also, some of the priorities (e.g., increasing the number of affordable and good quality early childcare institutions) may help to overcome barriers that young mothers from rural areas face, given that limited access to social support services is a great challenge, especially in rural areas. However, the official key indicators are missing to properly monitor the labour market situation of rural NEETs. This should be improved.

Finally, at the national level, the RYG policy framework includes measures for creating the institutional and structural conditions for NEETs employment and social integration. Specifically, national RYGs propose to tackle the barriers to labor market that NEETs face in all vulnerable areas, including in rural ones. These included limited job opportunities and limited access to educational and vocational training programs, making it hard to acquire the skills and qualifications necessary to compete in the labour market; limited access to public transportation, which can make it challenging for these young people to travel to nearby towns and cities for work, education, or other needs; or limited access to public childcare institutions which makes it difficult for young parents to reconcile work with family obligations.

4.5.1 New Research Developments

NEETs are defined mainly by age, employment and education (Arnett, 2007; Mascherini, 2019; Mauro & Mitra, 2020; Yates et al., 2011). An extensive research work is dedicated to youth employment and to policy frameworks addressing this issue. All this research work produces evidence for the improvement of the youth employment policy framework, including Youth Guarantee. Considering all the new developments of the EU and national policy framework on youth employment, in the following period there is a need, however, for new research avenues.

- **Impact evaluation for the RYG in each country.** Evaluations should be conducted regularly at the national and EU levels, and researchers should pay more attention to the urban-rural or regional disparities. Impact evaluation could analyse the individual and structural changes determined by RYG at national level.
- **Research on the new green and digital competences of young people.** This line of inquiry must include rural areas. The new integrated packages for NEETs cover training for green and digital skills, but it is important to see how these skills are applied.
- **Analysis of the active labour market policy instruments and their relevance in various EU contexts and for different NEETs categories.** The research of the ALMP instruments is important for the development and improvement of new policies.

4.5.2 Policy Implications

The analyses of RYG framework at national level shows the following improvements at policy level:

- **Prioritise the most vulnerable groups.** Many evaluations in various countries found that job seekers with better opportunities in the labour market are more likely to be included in programmes. The initiative should focus on the more vulnerable youth groups.
- **Address geographic disparities.** Flexibility should also be increased from a territorial perspective; remote, rural and peripheral authorities should be able to tailor the national program to local level context.
- **Tailored measures for different NEETs categories.** RYG proposes various measures for specific categories of NEETs (long term unemployed, people with disabilities, young people with family responsibilities, migrants etc). The individualised packages should be based on a needs analysis of NEETs and provide specific measures for various categories of NEETs. PES should be more flexible and implement these individualised packages.

References

Arnett, J. J. (2007). Emerging adulthood: What is it, and what is it good for? *Child Development Perspectives, 1*(2), 68–73.

Broeck, S., Hogarth, T., Baltina, L., & Lombardi, A. (2017). Skills Development and Employment: Apprenticeships, Internships and Volunteering. Study for the European Parliament's Committee on Employment and Social Affairs. *European Union.* https://www.europarl.europa.eu/RegData/etudes/STUD/2017/602056/IPOL_STU(2017)602056_EN.pdf

Bronfenbrenner, U. (1979). *The ecology of human development: Experiments by nature and design.* Harvard University Press.

Bronfenbrenner, U., & Evans, G. W. (2000). Developmental science in the 21st century: Emerging questions, theoretical models, research designs and empirical findings. *Social Development, 9*(1), 115–125.

Burlina, C., Crociata, A., & Odoardi, I. (2021). Can culture save young Italians? The role of cultural capital on Italian NEETs behaviour. *Economia Politica, 38*(3), 943–969. https://doi.org/10.1007/s40888-021-00219-7

Chinn, D., Klier, J., Stern, S., & Tesfu, S. (2020). *Safeguarding Europe's livelihoods: Mitigating the employment impact of COVID-19.* McKinsey. https://www.mckinsey.com/~/media/McKinsey/Industries/Public%20and%20Social%20Sector/Our%20Insights/Safeguarding%20Europes%20livelihoods%20Mitigating%20the%20employment%20impact%20of%20COVID%2019/Safeguarding-Europes-livelihoods-Mitigating-the-employment-impact-of-COVID-19-F.pdf

COUNCIL OF THE EUROPEAN UNION. (2021). *Council Resolution on a strategic framework for European cooperation in education and training towards the European Education Area and beyond (2021-2030)* (2021/C 66/01). Accessed June 21, 2023, from https://eur-lex.europa.eu/legal-content/EN/ALL/?uri=CELEX%3A32021G0226%2801%29

De Luca, G., Mazzocchi, P., Quintano, C., & Rocca, A. (2020). Going behind the high rates of NEETs in Italy and Spain: The role of early school leavers. *Social Indicators Research, 151*(1), 345–363. https://doi.org/10.1007/s11205-020-02370-3

Eurofound. (2016). *Exploring the diversity of NEETs.* Publications Office of the European Union.

Eurofound. (2020). *COVID-19 PolicyWatch.* Accessed June 20, 2023, from https://www.eurofound.europa.eu/data/covid-19-eu-policywatch

Eurofound. (2021). *Impact of COVID-19 on young people in the EU.* Publications Office of the European Union. Accessed June 20, 2023, https://www.eurofound.europa.eu/publications/report/2021/impact-of-covid-19-on-young-people-in-the-eu

European Commission. (2020a). COM(2020) 276 final. *Communication from the Commission to the European Parliament, the Council, the European Economic and Social Committee and the Committee of the Regions.* Accessed June 20, 2023, https://eur-lex.europa.eu/legal-content/EN/TXT/?qid=1594047420340&uri=CELEX%3A52020DC0276#footnote6

European Commission. (2020b). *Youth employment support: A bridge to jobs for the next generation.* Accessed June 20, 2023, https://eur-lex.europa.eu/legal-content/EN/TXT/?qid=1594047420340&uri=CELEX%3A52020DC0276

Eurostat. (2023). *Statistics on young people neither in employment nor in education or training.* Accessed June 2, 2023, https://ec.europa.eu/eurostat/statistics-explained/index.php?title=Statistics_on_young_people_neither_in_employment_nor_in_education_or_training#Does_it_matter_where_you_live.3F_A_glimpse_at_the_degree_of_urbanisation

Government of Hungary. (2014). *Hungary's National Youth Guarantee Implementation Plan.* https://ngmszakmaiteruletek.kormany.hu/download/9/4c/c0000/Youth%20Guarantee%20Implementation%20Plan.pdf

ILO. (2021). *World employment and social outlook: Trends 2021.* ILO. https://www.ilo.org/wcmsp5/groups/public/---dgreports/---dcomm/---publ/documents/publication/wcms_795453.pdf

ILO. (2022). *Global Employment Trends for Youth 2022: Investing in transforming futures for young people.* ILO. https://www.ilo.org/wcmsp5/groups/public/---dgreports/---dcomm/---publ/documents/publication/wcms_853321.pdf

Iruka, I. U., DeKraai, M., Walther, J., Sheridan, S. M., & Abdel-Monem, T. (2020). Examining how rural ecological contexts influence children's early learning opportunities. *Early Childhood Research Quarterly, 52*(3), 15–29. https://doi.org/10.1016/j.ecresq.2019.09.005

Koping-Tarki. (2021). *A munkaerő-piaci integrációt támogató konstrukciók értékelése.*

Lawy, R., Quinn, J., & Diment, K. (2010). Responding to the 'needs' of young people in jobs without training (JWT): some policy suggestions and recommendations. *Journal of Youth Studies, 13*(3), 335–352. https://doi.org/10.1080/13676260903447544

Lőrinc, M., Ryan, L., D'Angelo, A., & Kaye, N. (2020). De-individualising the 'NEET problem': An ecological systems analysis. *European Educational Research Journal, 19*(5), 412–427. https://doi.org/10.1177/1474904119880402

Madia, J. E., Obsuth, I., Thompson, I., Daniels, H., & Murray, A. L. (2022). Long-term labour market and economic consequences of school exclusions in England: Evidence from two counterfactual approaches. *British Journal of Educational Psychology, 92*(3), 801–816. https://doi.org/10.1111/bjep.12487

Mascherini, M. (2019). Origins and future of the concept of NEETs in the European policy agenda. In J. O'Reilly, J. Leschke, R. Ortlieb, M. Seeleib-Kaiser, & P. Villa (Eds.), *Comparing youth transitions in Europe: Joblessness, insecurity, and inequality* (pp. 503–529). Oxford Press.

Mauro Ellena, A., Marta, E., Simões, F., Fernandes-Jesus, M., & Petrescu, C. (2021). Soft skills and psychological well-being: A study on Italian rural and urban NEETs. *Calitatea Vieții, 32*(4), 352–370. https://doi.org/10.46841/RCV.2021.04.02

Mauro, J. A., & Mitra, S. (2020). Youth idleness in Eastern Europe and Central Asia before and after the 2009 crisis. *Applied Economics, 52*(15), 1634–1655. https://doi.org/10.1080/00036846.2019.1677848

Mukherjee, D. (2012). Schooling, child labor, and reserve army evidences from India. *Journal of Developing Societies, 28*(1), 1–29. https://doi.org/10.1177/0169796X1102800101

OECD. (2021). What have countries done to support young people in the COVID-19 crisis?, OECD policy responses to coronavirus (COVID-19), 6 July 2021. https://www.oecd.org/coronavirus/policy-responses/what-have-countries-done-to-support-young-people-in-the-covid-19-crisis-ac9f056c/

Petrescu, C., & Costantini, A. (Eds.). (2023). *Policy Report: Youth employment support services and advancing green job opportunities.* COST Action CA18213: Rural NEET Youth Network. https://rnyobservatory.eu/web/wp-content/uploads/2023/05/WG3-POLICY-REPORT-Youth-employment-support-services-and-advancing-green-job-opportunities.pdf

Petrescu, C., Ellena, A. M., Fernandes-Jesus, M., & Marta, E. (2022). Using evidence in policies addressing rural NEETs: Common patterns and differences in various EU countries. *Youth & Society, 54*(2_Suppl), 69S–88S. https://doi.org/10.1177/0044118X211056361

Petrescu, C., Neguț, A., & Mihalache, F. (2021). Implementation of the Youth Guarantee Programme in Romania. *Calitatea Vieții, 32*(4), 449–467. https://doi.org/10.46841/RCV.2021.04.07

Petrescu, C., & Prieto-Flores, O. (Eds.). (2023). *Employment and employment services for rural NEETs: Initiatives for tackling NEETs' and rural NEETs' employment issues.* COST Action CA 18213: Rural NEET Youth Network: Modeling the risks underlying rural NEETs social exclusion. https://rnyobservatory.eu/web/wp-content/uploads/2023/03/REPORT-WG3-Employment-and-Employment-Services-for-Rural.pdf

Public Employment Service Estatal (SEPE). (2021). *Spain. Youth Guarantee Plan Plus 2021 – 2027 of decent work for young people.* https://www.sepe.es/HomeSepe/en/Personas/encontrartrabajo/Garantia-Juvenil/plan-garantia-juvenil-plus.html

Sadler, K., Akister, J., & Burch, S. (2015). Who are the young people who are not in education, employment or training? An application of the risk factors to a rural area in the UK. *International Social Work, 58*(4), 508–520. https://doi.org/10.1177/0020872813515010

Simões, F. (2022). *School to work transition in the Resilience and Recovery Facility framework: Youth oriented active labour market policies under Pillar 6.* Publications Office of the European Union. http://www.europarl.europa.eu/supporting-analyses

Simões, F., Meneses, A., Luís, R., & Drumonde, R. (2017). NEETs in a rural region of Southern Europe: Perceived self-efficacy, perceived barriers, educational expectations, and vocational expectations. *Journal of Youth Studies, 20*(9), 1109–1126. https://doi.org/10.1080/13676261.2017.1311403

Smoter, M. (2022). Outreach practices of public employment services targeted at NEET youth in Poland. *Youth & Society, 54*(2_Suppl), 89S–108S. https://doi.org/10.1177/0044118X211058224

Yates, S., Harris, A., Sabates, R., & Staff, J. (2011). Early occupational aspirations and fractured transitions: A study of entry into 'NEET' status in the UK. *Journal of Social Policy, 40*(3), 513–534. https://doi.org/10.1017/S0047279410000656

Open Access This chapter is licensed under the terms of the Creative Commons Attribution 4.0 International License (http://creativecommons.org/licenses/by/4.0/), which permits use, sharing, adaptation, distribution and reproduction in any medium or format, as long as you give appropriate credit to the original author(s) and the source, provide a link to the Creative Commons license and indicate if changes were made.

The images or other third party material in this chapter are included in the chapter's Creative Commons license, unless indicated otherwise in a credit line to the material. If material is not included in the chapter's Creative Commons license and your intended use is not permitted by statutory regulation or exceeds the permitted use, you will need to obtain permission directly from the copyright holder.

Chapter 5
Pathways for Young Farmers' Entrepreneurship in Sustainable Rural Development

Alen Mujčinović, Štefan Bojnec, Aleksandra Nikolić, Anita Bušljeta Tonković, Slaven Gašparović, Messaoud Lazereg, Anđelka Stojanović, and Daniela Bojadjieva

Abstract In this chapter we develop a theoretical-conceptual model on young farmers' entrepreneurship in multi-functional, diverse and resilient sustainable rural development. Our aim is supported by policies fostering social and economic opportunities that target both rural youth and rural female entrepreneurship. The European Green Deal and associated targeted initiatives offer new avenues for agriculture, rural development, and social innovation aiming at vulnerable youth groups in rural communities such as rural young people Not in Employment, not in Education or Training (NEETs), or at setting up new, viable, and attractive businesses for overcoming negative representations about farming among rural younger generations. We identify and explain the obstacles and the policy opportunities for stronger rural youth entrepreneurship and their contribution to sustainable rural development. We make this by considering the concepts of sustainability and resilience associated with the multifunctionality and heterogeneity of rural areas in

---

A. Mujčinović (✉) · A. Nikolić
Faculty of Agriculture and Food Sciences, University of Sarajevo, Sarajevo, Bosnia and Herzegovina
e-mail: a.mujcinovic@ppf.unsa.ba

Š. Bojnec
Faculty of Management, University of Primorska, Koper-Capodistria, Slovenia

A. B. Tonković
Ivo Pilar Institute of Social Sciences, Regional Centre Gospic, Gospic, Croatia

S. Gašparović
Faculty of Science, Department of Geography, University of Zagreb, Zagreb, Croatia

M. Lazereg
Research Centre in Applied Economics for Development, Algiers, Algeria

A. Stojanović
Technical Faculty in Bor, University of Belgrade, Bor, Serbia

D. Bojadjieva
Faculty of Economics, Ss. Cyril and Methodius University in Skopje, Skopje, North Macedonia

© The Author(s) 2024
F. Simões, E. Erdogan (eds.), *NEETs in European rural areas*, SpringerBriefs in Sociology, https://doi.org/10.1007/978-3-031-45679-4_5

the context of the Industry 4.0 uprising. Altogether, these elements can determine young people's level of involvement in the farming sector and their willingness to stay in rural areas, including among the most vulnerable ones. We also provide a set of research avenues to overcome traditional farming approaches and policy recommendations fostering entrepreneurship among rural young people.

Keywords Sustainability · Resilience · Rural development · Rural-urban continuum · Social economy · Green employment · Entrepreneurship

5.1 Introduction

Rural areas cover 44.6% of the total European Union (EU) territory, accounting for almost 30% of its population. These territories play an important role in economic growth, social pluralism, and the well-being of the population while promoting environmental aesthetics (EU 2021). In line with developments in other parts of the world, the EU has experienced a rural decline reflected in relatively high rates of youth migration and social exclusion (Farrugia, 2016). However, economic and social conditions are more favorable in urban areas and have resulted in improved youth development trajectories, which ultimately results in a shrinkage of rural economies, and adverse social consequences, in particular for rural youth (Bæck, 2016; Farrugia, 2016). Currently, global challenges and a rapidly evolving societal landscape require a concerted effort to support different and diverse community-led interventions that can result in resilient, flexible, and adaptive communities, especially in rural areas (Simões et al., 2021). Within such a movement, one that seeks to find a sustainable development pathway for rural areas, young people must play an important role in the design and implementation of innovative solutions if they are to benefit from the resultant opportunities which are intended to shape their development trajectories. Therefore, it is important to ignite discussion about the conditions to promote the capacity of young people to take a more central role in the social transformation of rural areas in order to inform and improve public policies that can ensure potent youth development trajectories (Simões et al., 2023).

Thus, in this chapter, we aim to develop a conceptual model around pathways for young farmers' entrepreneurship and its contribution to sustainable rural development, including for vulnerable groups of rural young people such as those Not in Employment Nor in Education or Training (NEET) and young women. Our approach touches all levels of the bioecological model (Bronfenbrenner & Evans, 2000) from policies to practices of rural young people. Therefore, an ecological approach is applied to multifunctional and sustainable rural development. Our goal is justified by four arguments. Firstly, to capture the complexity of rural development and the formation of youth development trajectories it is critical to understand the multi-functionality and heterogeneity of rural areas, and the need to make them more sustainable and resilient. Secondly, new approaches based on the use of new technologies, from the so-called Industry 4.0, can lead to the identification of visible and less visible factors upholding the potential of young farmers to benefit from existing social and economic opportunities. In other words, Industry 4.0 can stimulate innovation in rural economies/agribusiness, thus transforming it into a modern ecosystem within the digital landscape of the rural-urban continuum. Thirdly, there is a need to discuss and coordinate a set of diverse current policy options in order to improve young farmers' entrepreneurship. These policies focus on rural development and entrepreneurship, aiming to foster social and economic opportunities, with a particular emphasis on rural youth and female entrepreneurship aiming to overcome the negative representation of farming among these groups. With this in mind, our approach combines a series of case studies describing public interventions that are relevant in the rural development field (Mujčinović & Bojnec, 2023). Finally, our chapter focuses on social initiatives that can help facilitate the transition towards sustainable rural development, including improved future prospects for rural youth. In conclusion, the need to innovate in all aspects of rural life is underlined while explaining the multi-faceted problem of innovation diffusion.

After undertaking our theoretical exploration, we offer a set of recommendations to shed some light on the urgent need for policy interventions supporting rural youth entrepreneurship. These interventions should be more focused on real-world impact, more inclusive, and reflect the multi-faceted challenges of building prosperous rural ecosystems connected with urban areas in both physical and digital landscapes. Our recommendations follow the principle that all public policies should promote the concept of neo-endogenous development aiming to strengthen the integral development of the local community. This can be achieved by making the best use of local human and natural resources, including local customs or culture, heritage, and geography. Moreover, our recommendations rely on typical endogenous resources and on the cooperation of residents, local stakeholders, and governmental organizations for strengthening the common will and cultural self-confidence of the local residents, including marginalized groups such as NEETs or rural women.

5.2 Sustainability, Resilience, and Multi-functionality Towards Diverse Rural Areas: Creating a Rural-Urban Continuum

To capture how young farmers' trajectories can be better supported in contemporary rural areas, it is important to understand three interconnected concepts which are key for these territories: sustainability, resilience, and multifunctionality. From our point of view, such concepts are inseparable and indispensable. Sustainability is defined as "meeting the needs of the present without compromising the ability of future generations to meet their own needs" (UN, 1987). It is a holistic approach that considers ecological, social, and economic dimensions, needed to assure wellbeing for all. In turn, resilience is the capacity of a system to resist, absorb, adapt, transform, and recover from shocks (Walker & Pearson, 2007). Building upon sustainability and resilience notions, multifunctionality essentially 'maps' the functional relationships underlying rural development processes and provides insight into the specific reconfigurations in the use of resources such as land, labor, knowledge, and nature (Knickel & Renting, 2000).

Rural areas are complex units, consisting of many elements and several interactions between those elements inside and outside their ecosystem. These interactions also involve interactions between sustainability, resilience, and multifunctionality which can take many forms. For instance, the resilience of rural communities depends on the sustainability of many elements such as the economy, population, social networks, spatial factors, public policies, etc. (Roberts et al., 2017). Moreover, the levels of policy responses have paid limited attention to the diverse, multi-sectoral, and multi-functional attributes of rural areas further shaping the resilience and sustainability levels of each rural community (Knickel & Renting, 2000). These two examples illustrate that there is no single "model" for achieving sustainable rural development. Indeed, many rural areas struggle to be perceived as attractive and stimulating environments resulting in a vast number of policy interventions, measures, and action plans being introduced to mitigate and reverse negative trends associated with rural areas.

Recent research suggests a need to change the perception of rural areas as "agricultural dominant", "isolated", and "traditional" in terms of doing business. Policy interventions focused on understanding rural areas have been and will continue to be important, if not critical, in preserving the landscape and promoting a shift towards sustainable development and well-being for all (IFAD, 2019). However, at the same time, up-trending elements such as the so-called Industry 4.0, must be taken into account in the process of changing the representation and livelihoods of rural areas. By Industry 4.0 we mean cutting-edge technologies (Zareiyan & Korjani, 2018) that connect cyber and physical objects with the main agenda to enhance the level of data generation, usage, and information integration across the supply chain (Esmaeilian et al., 2020). These processes result in creating an engaging interactive automated activities (Sestino et al., 2020) focused on intelligent, anticipative, self-organizing, self-structuring business processes allowing value generation and innovative services (Esmaeilian et al., 2020) which ultimately improve quality of life for all, including in rural areas (Nikolić et al., 2022a, 2022b). According to the European Commission (2023), Industry 4.0 and the digital technologies underpinning it have "the potential to revolutionize the industry, promoting efficiency, sustainability, and competitiveness." The benefits of digital technologies coming from Industry 4.0 are expected to make farming jobs more attractive to young people (Alarcón-Ferrari et al., 2023), providing role models with risk-taking values and agency in rural areas for vulnerable young (rural NEETs, female ones in particular) (Simões, 2018; Simões & Rio, 2020), but also to offer them the possibility of finding attractive "urban" jobs without having to leave rural areas. Still, digital inequality, which is the digital under-serving of certain areas, affects young rural people by reducing the availability of access to the necessary information and therefore to seize the employment opportunities provided by digitalization (Philip & Williams, 2019). The severity of the digital divide was highlighted during the COVID-19 pandemic resulting in a deepening of pre-existing social gaps between

5 Pathways for Young Farmers' Entrepreneurship in Sustainable...

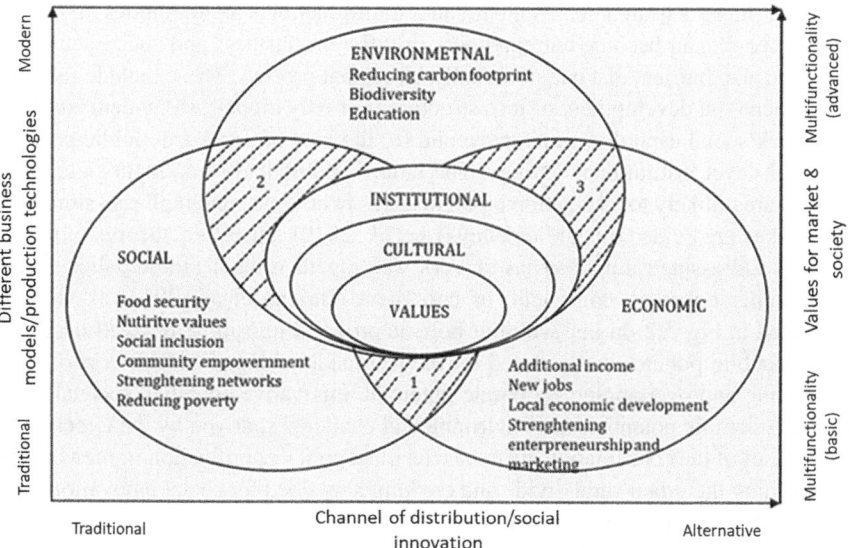

Fig. 5.1 Sustainability and Multi-functionality—creating value for all (Nikolić et al., 2022a, 2022b)

rural and urban areas (Lai & Widmar, 2021). Likewise, the pandemic also demonstrated the importance of resilient rural communities and food supply chains (Aday & Aday, 2020).

Our holistic approach to the rural economy, combining sustainability, resilience, and multifunctionality, in a period of intense technological changes, is graphically depicted in Fig. 5.1. Our proposal can build a new rural environment in which the cyber, physical, and social environments are integrated. Such an environment is attractive and is characterized by multiple outcomes also listed in Fig. 5.1. These outcomes can be located at the environmental (e.g., reducing carbon footprint), social (e.g., food security), or economic (e.g., new jobs) levels, bringing value to both the market and the society, thus generating well-being for all. Moreover, our proposed approach for value creation in rural areas has the potential to generate a new ecosystem for reducing the importance of location while building a new urban-rural continuum (Nikolić et al., 2022a, 2022b). Moreover, our holistic view of rural areas has also been advanced in the literature focused on alternative food systems such as research on business model "care farms" that combine agricultural production with healthcare and social services (Hassink et al., 2016). Thus, in a nutshell, and in light of the current challenges to increase the sustainability of rural communities, it appears reasonable to develop a single integrated socio-economic system ("ecosystem") that bridges the existing urban-rural divide and emphasizes economic, social, and environmental sustainability.

How are policies supporting our holistic vision? While the EU's strategies and initiatives for rural transformation include several elements that can potentially facilitate more sustainable, resilient, and multifunctional communities in which young people can become entrepreneurs in different business and social activities, there are also barriers that can potentially block that process. These include (a) poor investment and development of infrastructure (not only digital); (b) underdeveloped and weak social capital in rural areas; and (c) the lack of consistent public policies and high-level institutional settings. The latter is particularly important since individuals are unlikely to take action by themselves in complex and high-risk situations unless they are guided by public policy (Li et al., 2019). Therefore, the mix of public policies addressing rural areas has to work well together, that is, these policies have to be either coherent, consistent, or congruent (Bazzan et al., 2023) as visually presented in Fig. 5.2. In line with our holistic proposal transition to a well-designed mix of public policies is illustrated on the right side of Fig. 5.2. This sort of mix, combining and overlapping economic potential, innovative potential, societal challenges, scientific potential, and environmental challenges, driven by the Green Deal at the heart of the coordination efforts, is the ideal policy coordination framework for overcoming the urban-rural divide and creating a seedbed for social innovations and creative business ideas led by young farmers and entrepreneurs, which can contribute to sustainable and resilient rural communities.

5.3 Challenges and Barriers for Young Farmers' Entrepreneurship

Farming is a complex, unpredictable, and often individual business where farmers must meet the changing needs of our planet as well as the expectations of regulators, environmentalists, consumers, food processors, and retailers. Young farmers also face increasing pressures of climate change, soil erosion, and biodiversity loss. In addition, young farmers must consider consumers' changing tastes in food and concerns about how it is produced. All of the aforementioned considerations require different approaches and innovative responses that are either product, process, or management-related/oriented. Multi-functional attributes of agriculture can be seen as a solution to support young farmers, but multi-functionality in rural areas is not easy to achieve (Hassinik et al., 2016). There is a need for changing the approach of the involved stakeholders for supporting young farmers' entrepreneurship, in order to redefine capacities, strategies, practices, interrelations, and networks (Van der Ploeg et al., 2000). New institutional arrangements and professional structures are needed (Renting et al., 2008) with the establishment of new forms and mechanisms of communication, collaboration, and coordination between young farmers and the wider society (Hassinik et al., 2016).

However, the traditional way of doing business in rural areas is difficult to abandon (Burton & Wilson, 2006) as it requires new skills and knowledge, which are often not readily provided by traditional support systems (Renting et al., 2008). Strong bonds in rural areas cannot be seen as a disadvantage in stimulating the

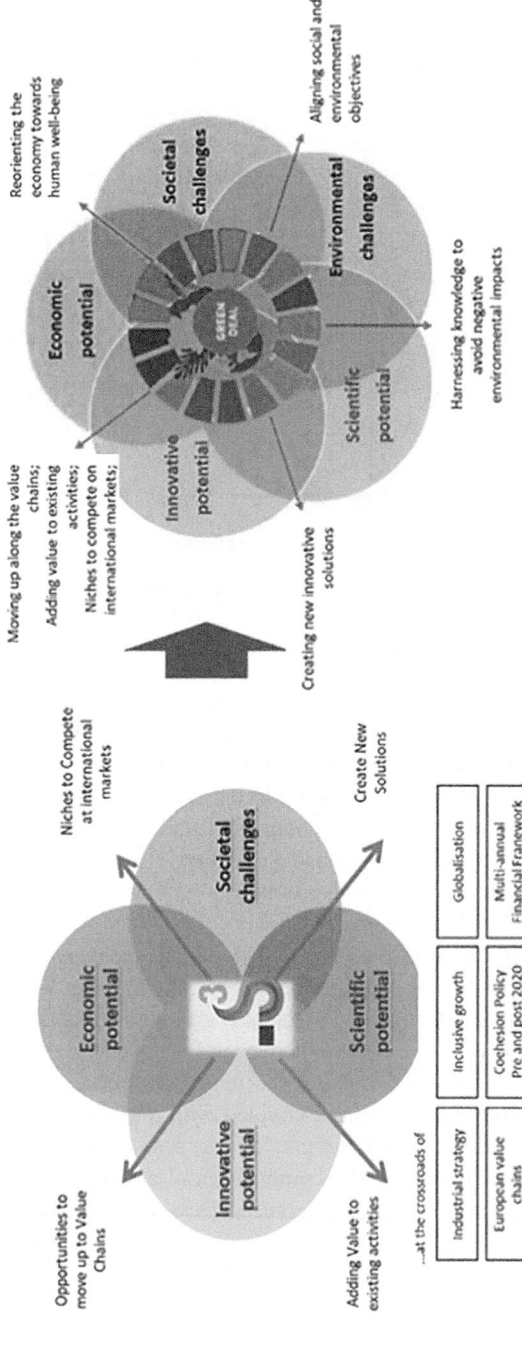

Fig. 5.2 Framework for public policies and interventions in youth development (Gnamus, 2021)

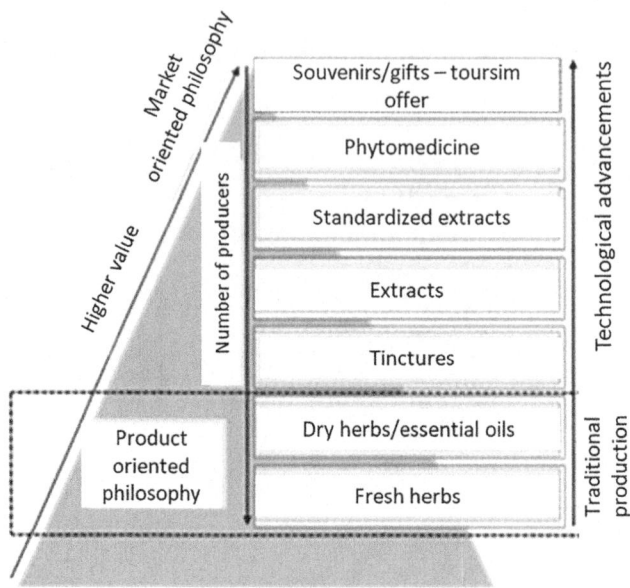

Fig. 5.3 Value pyramid and current production capacity in Bosnia and Herzegovina (Mujčinović, 2020)

development of new and innovative business practices. In turn, they need to be enriched with entrepreneurial training/programs/interventions (Seuneke et al., 2013) followed by the creation of new types of networks (bridging and linking), rules, and regulations (Ruvio & Shoham, 2011). Networking is seen as especially important to discover opportunities for increasing economies of scale, securing resources, developing knowledge, and gaining legitimacy (Hekkert et al., 2007), especially for young people from non-farming backgrounds or young newcomers (McGreevy et al., 2019; Simões, 2018; Simões et al., 2021).

In addition, family succession is still the dominant pathway into the farming sector but with ever-decreasing importance. Indeed, the existing literature suggests that the number of young newcomers with no background in agriculture is increasing significantly (EIP-AGRI, 2016). Part of the reason for the decreasing importance of family succession in farming lies behind the uncertain trajectory of conventional agriculture that discourages succession, coupled with a growing interest in multifunctional agriculture (Berti, 2020) and greater openness to different approaches to farming and off-farm activities i.e. the combination of agricultural production with healthcare and social services of the newcomers (Dessein et al., 2013). This combination of factors with the intention to provide added-value products is more usually seen among young farmers. Figure 5.3 provides an example of this approach with a case study of medicinal and aromatic plant producers in Bosnia and Herzegovina (Mujčinović, 2020).

According to Fig. 5.3, traditionally, farmers tend to produce minimum value-added products, because of low interest in innovating production techniques as well as generally lower skills that would allow them technological and business advancements. So in this case, traditional farmers are more inclined to produce fresh/dry herbs or essential oils. On the contrary, newcomers are more prone to experiment and innovate and more willing to start sustainable farming practices (Padel, 2001; EIP-AGRI, 2016), including orientation toward alternative food networks as a new market opportunity (Laforge & Levkoe, 2018). In the illustrated case they are more inclined to produce souvenirs and gifts for tourists.

5.4 Opportunities in Policy Options

Facing the potential negative consequences of rural depopulation and the importance of balanced regional development in European countries, there is an increasing willingness to invest in more opportunities targeting the rural youth population. Policy options that can facilitate sustainable, resilient, and multifunctional rural areas are aiming to support alternative marketing channels to strengthen the role of short food supply chains (SFSCs), rural women empowerment and entrepreneurship, and young farmers (Ball, 2020; Laforge & Levkoe, 2018). We systematize the existing policy opportunities in four domains: EU policy framework, territorial development, synergy and networking, and creativity and social innovation.

5.4.1 EU Policy Framework for Rural Development

Different EU strategic documents such as the Long Term Vision for Rural Areas and more recently a Rural Pact and Rural Action Plan have addressed challenges in rural development (EC, 2021a). At the core of EU policies for rural development and of other more transversal EU policies such as the Green Deal, is innovation and support for innovation and entrepreneurship (EC, 2019). Indeed, within the Youth Strategy 2019–2027, the EU has acknowledged the importance of gender equality and support for young people living in rural areas (EU, 2018). Furthermore, the Commission emphasizes green and digital transition as the basis of youth employment policies in the future. The Digital Agenda for Europe 2020–2030, focuses on the changes taking place under the influence of digital technologies, especially in the business field (EC, 2021b). The 2030 Digital Compass, proposed by the EU in 2021, represents a set of goals to be met by 2030 with the potential to empower people and businesses in the direction of a sustainable society in the future (EC, 2021c).

5.4.2 Territorial Development: Funding Mechanisms

The successful absorption of EU funds can depend on different factors such as the ability to co-finance and refund human resources required in project preparation, the level of skills of project developers to comply with the complexity of procedures or the actual implementation of funded projects. Agricultural economics literature focuses particularly on instruments and measures of the Common Agricultural Policy (CAP) and its two pillars: Pillar I for direct payments to farmers and Pillar II for rural development with support for farming in more vulnerable areas, support for voluntary adoption of agri-environmental farming practices (i.e. Agri-Environmental Schemes—AESs), support for farms undergoing restructuring, including diversification into non-agricultural activities, and restructuring in rural development (Unay-Gailhard & Bojnec, 2019). The renewal of farms, the empowerment of highly qualified young farmers, and the creation of jobs can be an important set of measures of CAP Pillar II for bringing in more young farmers to the sector who are often more educated, and more in line with the sustainable, resilient and multifunctional perspective for rural areas.

5.4.3 Synergy and Networking: Success Factors of the Policy Interventions

There are examples of successful practices where rural areas were in a disadvantaged position and managed to turn around their socioeconomic situation by boosting development actors' synergies. There is a consensus that those regions realize that success cannot be generated exclusively at the local level or imposed by the regional and/or national and international (EU) level policies. Instead, local synergies, making the most of natural and human resources, and meeting bottom-up initiatives with top-down approaches are key to achieving desirable outcomes, including in terms of promoting younger farmers' entrepreneurship. The Neo-Endogenous Development (NED) perspective is considered a promising bottom-up, participatory, or joint development approach to promote local synergies and networking (Ray, 2001). This conceptual standpoint, potentially applicable to any sub-national (both rural and urban) geographical area, is shaped through three basic assumptions. First, NED suggests that local development is better stimulated by focusing on the particular needs of specific rural territories and their communities, including a shift from the classical analysis of needs to targeting individual sectors of the economy. Second, NED postulates that development and overall economic activities are reorganized to valorize and use endogenous resources, both natural and human, thus retaining as many potential benefits as possible in the local area. Third, development is contextualized by focusing on the needs, capacities, and perspectives of the local population. Namely, this development model also assumes an ethical dimension by emphasizing the principles and processes of local participation in the design and implementation of a particular action, especially through the adoption of cultural, environmental, and common values as part of a particular development intervention (Ray, 2001). This includes young people and local citizens (bottom-up approach), i.e., their needs (in economic, social, and cultural terms), and integrating the visions of the key local, regional, and state developmental actors (top-down approach). This is the space where the bottom-up and top-down approaches should meet. Thus, the human, social, cultural, and especially natural capital of a certain community in a specific rural area and how these resources are connected with each other is considered a key element of development that can foster youth farming entrepreneurship.

5.4.4 Creativity and Social Innovation: "New" Agrifood Opportunities

The agri-food sector is very competitive and characterized by unsustainable practices aiming strongly for innovations as a source of continuous growth and competitive advantage for companies (De Medeiros et al., 2014). Sustainability and multi-functionality of rural areas involving on-farm and off-farm employment activities are desirable and constitute a "must" approach in the twenty-first century (Knickel & Renting, 2000). The multi-functionality of the sector is explained through the service sector activities in rural areas that have expanded very rapidly. As agriculture and industry shrink, a rise of on- and off-farm non-farming employment activities and incomes in areas such as farm tourism or the integration of care services into farms become more prominent, representing an opportunity for rural young people—from entrepreneurs to rural youth in greater need (Hassink et al., 2016).

Over the last four decades, the importance of AESs as voluntary tools to enhance the rural environment beyond legal requirements has greatly increased, in terms of expenditure and participation (Riley, 2016). AESs sometimes need a long period to produce the desired environmental benefits, often beyond the ordinary contract duration (Swetnam et al., 2004). In addition, they may require relevant changes to farming practices, resulting in more complex and lengthy decision-making patterns (Defrancesco et al., 2018). Once accomplished, adoption should then be accompanied by steady behavioral changes (Reimer et al., 2014), while early withdrawals from the schemes may jeopardize or even nullify the AESs' long-term success (Riley, 2016). Because of a significant decrease in the number of farmers across the world, there is an urgent need to diversify rural livelihoods. Rural livelihood diversification indicates the process by which rural households construct an increasingly diverse portfolio of activities and assets to survive and improve their standard of living (Ellis, 2000). In developed countries, rural diversification is not only about complementing on-farm activities but also with new, off-farm, non-agricultural activities. It is also the case that creating a new foundation for the local rural economy, in which local agriculture merely is part of the mix, driven by responsible consumption and customers' need to support the health and well-being of the individual, family, and community.

For example, 96% of EU farms in agriculture are family-run, but women manage only 28% of them (EU, 2021). To support gender equality in rural areas, greater rural women empowerment is needed with more knowledge insights to be produced through the provision of more comprehensive gender-disaggregated data on the participation of women in agricultural and other rural entrepreneurial activities and on the factors inhibiting or hampering wider participation. As observed in other sectors, education, gender stereotyping, lack of confidence, and difficulties in reconciling work and family obligations are at the root of lower female participation. When it comes to rural areas, problems accessing resources (e.g., land, finance, and business networks) along with patriarchal inheritance practices, are the key barriers to women-led agriculture and enterprise. There is also a need to improve our understanding and recognition of women's role in contributing to environmental protection due to their more sustainable attitudes and behaviors as well as more socially inclusive practices. Women can be at the forefront of environmentally sustainable farming practices, such as organic farming, small-scale extensive farming, and localized supply chains (Ball, 2020). Based on research results, more effective policy and governance frameworks can be formulated both to support and build female participation in rural areas and to exploit women's potential and contribution to rural regeneration. Despite the requirement for gender mainstreaming in EU policy, gaps still exist. Shortall (2015) analyses this in the CAP context showing that policy advances focus on gender inequality symptoms rather than the causes. The targeting of policy measures towards creating a supporting infrastructure for innovative female-led sustainable and climate-resilient farming and food production is a necessary action.

5.5 Conclusion

Global challenges and dramatic social changes call attention to the need for new and viable business and social activities in rural areas while breaking down the locked-in pattern of existing socio-economic relations and traditional ways of "doing business". Young farmers and their development trajectory are seen as key ingredients of this process of radical change for this to happen. With this chapter, we aim to develop a conceptual model around pathways for young farmers' entrepreneurship in multi-functional, diverse, and resilient sustainable rural development. Our approach was based on all levels of the bioecological model—from policies to rural young people. Such an approach shed light on the holistic characteristics of rural areas where sustainable and multifunctional rural areas can stimulate transformation, boost young farmers' entrepreneurship, and build a new environment in which cyber, physical, and social environments are integrated through the radical changes based on new technologies (Industry 4.0).

To enable young people to be actors in a radical transformation of the rural ecosystem, it is important to take care of the typical mismatch between youth aspirations and available opportunities as well as the mismatch between youth skills and available jobs. This is typically driven by young people's (rural NEETs and women in particular) negative perception of rural areas as being marginalised, obsolete and unattractive territories. Therefore, capacity building of rural youth entrepreneurship must consider that all rural interventions have to touch and positively influence the agricultural perceptions and attitudes of youth throughout their whole life especially through early exposure to agricultural experiences and career paths during the middle and high school years (Jean-Philippe et al., 2017). Our holistic approach for upholding young farmers' entrepreneurship that can represent opportunities for vulnerable, rural young people as well should be based on the strong promotion of a positive image of rural areas: nature, the culture of life—"everyone knows everyone", peace, solidarity, and spirit of cooperation, beautiful, cosy, quiet, and pleasant by part of the local youth, cultural heritage, clean and ethical food, space and peace and experiences. The development of young farmers' entrepreneurship and rural community capacity to innovate requires mechanisms to expose all actors to a broad range of new ideas and opportunities provided by the policies that we have listed. These include, for instance, synergies and networking between local actors or creativity and innovation in many different ways such as the promotion of alternative marketing channels such as short food supply chains (including new business models). Altogether, these factors can uphold rural entrepreneurship, including among specific youth groups such as rural women and or NEETs.

5.5.1 New Research Developments

To sum up, we suggest some ideas contributing to new research agendas that can contribute to young farmer's entrepreneurship trajectories, based on relevant insights for NGOs, policymakers, and communities collected under the COST Action Rural NEET Youth Network (Mujčinović & Bojnec, 2023).

- **Better understanding of the alternative marketing channels and the role of Short Food Supply Chains (SFSC) in youth empowerment/engagement**. Communication with consumers and building trust through precise rules of conduct (good agricultural practices), certification, and the communication of strategically important information (about cultivation methods, technology, processing/finishing) places SFSCs at the centre of business, and guarantees business sustainability (Kneafsey et al., 2013). SFSCs have numerous positive impacts on economic, environmental, and social sustainability, or health (product quality and general well-being). SFSCs contribute to the reconnection of producers and consumers which results in a higher level of trust, and subsequently influences the decision to purchase products from short chains (Holloway &

Kneafsey, 2000). SFSC can catalyse rural development by providing added value to local environments, and creating new economic systems (Van der Ploeg et al., 2000), and also preventing the loss of ecosystem services and agricultural infrastructure (Canfora, 2016). However, all of these effects still need to be better addressed in the context of young farmers' entrepreneurship.

- **Understanding rural female empowerment and rural entrepreneurship is critical.** Female entrepreneurs, and female entrepreneurship in general, are gaining importance year by year, and have been recognized as a source of new business opportunities, as well as a means to achieving economic growth and development. In addition to the basic creation of new business opportunities, economic growth, and development. Female entrepreneurs also contribute to the diversification of business activities within economic systems giving them the opportunity to express and realize their full potential (Verheul et al., 2006). Numerous factors influencing female entrepreneurship have been identified in the literature, such as human capital (education and work experience) (Carter et al., 2003); cultural problems (Ufuk & Özgen, 2001); a lack of funds (Manolova et al., 2007); and, belonging to different formal and informal networks (Manolova et al., 2007). A detailed overview of why females may have been neglected, and how their approaches to farming may differ, is presented by Schmidt et al. (2021) and should be used to build up solutions and interventions to activate women's potential while promoting new business models such as green, circular, shared economy or services connected to access infrastructure (ICT and other types). We suggest that the Green Deal and agri-environmental measures should be more strategically used to promote women's entrepreneurship because recent review studies (i.e., Ball, 2020) conclude that women farmers demonstrate greater sensitivity towards agri-environmental farming practices and are more involved with sustainable farming practices, such as organic farming, and alternative agriculture practices compared to male farmers. This is highlighted in many articles and policy briefs, but agriculture remains seen as a "male" dominant activity, contributing to the subsequent masculinization of rural areas across many European countries. Adding to this, most of the research is focused on female entrepreneurship in general, but not in rural areas. In addition to that, because of the growing interest in female entrepreneurship, new approaches/ methodological perspectives should be used to better understand and capture this issue.

- **Understanding challenges and obstacles of the young farmers and NEETs and their ability to modernize rural areas.** Previous studies have documented that younger farmers are usually more progressive and flexible in the adoption of new sustainable technologies compared to their older counterparts who tend to be more comfortable with traditional practices (Salazar et al., 2019). Moreover, older farmers are more risk-averse, use fewer sources of information than their younger colleagues, are less willing to experiment, have shorter planning windows, and are more focused on the financial performance of their farms (Brown et al., 2019). At the same time, young farmers may be more familiar with new technologies as they have better knowledge to optimally operate information-intensive technologies and, therefore, are more willing to adopt new technology (Barnes et al., 2019). Therefore, the support of young farmers is at the heart of agribusiness transformation and development of a new digital landscape that diminishes the role of location building rural-urban continuum offering attractive jobs on and off farms and within rural and urban areas. It is important to understand, then, how young farmers' entrepreneurship is contributing to greater social inclusion in rural areas by, for instance, creating new job opportunities in farming for vulnerable people, including rural NEETs.

5.5.2 Policy Recommendations

Our policy recommendations take into consideration the scope and objectives of the paper and keep in mind the complexity and heterogeneity of the rural areas which requires tailor-made policy options/actions. Policies in this domain have to be long-term, coherent, and well-promoted, including the mechanisms to support networking, the development of trust and reciprocity, and the build-up of local social networks. Social innovations upholding young farmers' entrepreneurship have to be developed based on technological innovations leading to new social relationships covering all actors, public policies, and resources embedded within the socioeconomic relations of rural areas. In this context, two pathways for policy interventions are offered to induce the development of rural, community-based food systems within the digital landscape of the future.

- **Foster and promote sustainable economic growth in rural areas.** This line of action requires in-depth assessing of the current measures/policies/action plans and raising awareness of the need to use mixed approaches in designing and implementing public policies and aligning with youth needs and capabilities in rural areas. This also implies investments into the rural infrastructure for improving the quality of life and in particular to digital infrastructure in rural areas while at the same time improving the digital skills among the rural youth and rural population in general to induce digital transformation.
- **Promotions and diffusion of new, modern, and innovative activities (business models).** Here we consider measures for the production of high-quality and region-specific products, product brand development, nature conservation and landscape management, agritourism, and the development of short-supply chains. Such activities should also be followed by a strong promotion of a positive image of rural areas aiming to attract new technology/practice adopters (newcomers) along the value chain. This goal can be achieved through applying networked rural development models that are locally established focusing on local capacity-building or early childhood exposure to agricultural experiences, among other complementary activities in rural areas.

References

Aday, S., & Aday, M. S. (2020). Impact of COVID-19 on the food supply chain. *Food Quality and Safety, 4*(4), 167–180. https://doi.org/10.1093/fqsafe/fyaa024

Alarcón-Ferrari, C., Corrado, A., & Fama, M. (2023). Digitalisation, politics of sustainability and new agrarian questions: The case of dairy farming in rural spaces of Italy and Sweden. *Sociologia Ruralis*. https://doi.org/10.1111/soru.12420

Bæck, U.-D. K. (2016). Rural location and academic success: Remarks on research, contextualisation and methodology. *Scandinavian Journal of Educational Research, 60*(4), 435–448. https://doi.org/10.1080/00313831.2015.1024163

Ball, J. A. (2020). Women farmers in developed countries: A literature review. *Agriculture and Human Values, 37*(2), 147–160. https://doi.org/10.1007/s10460-019-09978-3

Barnes, A. P., Soto, I., Eory, V., Beck, B., Balafoutis, A., Sánchez, B., et al. (2019). Exploring the adoption of precision agricultural technologies: A cross regional study of EU farmers. *Land Use Policy, 80*, 163–174. https://doi.org/10.1016/j.landusepol.2018.10.004

Bazzan, G., Daugbjerg, C., & Tosun, J. (2023). Attaining policy integration through the integration of new policy instruments: The case of the Farm to Fork Strategy. *Applied Economic Perspectives and Policy, 45*(2), 803–818. https://doi.org/10.1002/aepp.13235

Berti, G. (2020). Sustainable agri-food economies: Re-territorialising farming practices, markets, supply chains, and policies. *Agriculture, 10*(3), 64. https://doi.org/10.3390/agriculture10030064

Bronfenbrenner, U., & Evans, G. W. (2000). Developmental science in the 21st century: Emerging questions, theoretical models, research designs and empirical findings. *Social Development, 9*(1), 115–125.

Brown, P., Daigneault, A., & Dawson, J. (2019). Age, values, farming objectives, past management decisions, and future intentions in New Zealand agriculture. *Journal of Environmental Management, 231*, 110–120. https://doi.org/10.1016/j.jenvman.2018.10.018

Burton, R. J., & Wilson, G. A. (2006). Injecting social psychology theory into conceptualisations of agricultural agency: Towards a post-productivist farmer self-identity? *Journal of Rural Studies, 22*(1), 95–115. https://doi.org/10.1016/j.jrurstud.2005.07.004

Canfora, I. (2016). Is the short food supply chain an efficient solution for sustainability in food market? *Agriculture and Agricultural Science Procedia, 8*, 402–407. https://doi.org/10.1016/j.aaspro.2016.02.036

Carter, N. M., & Williams, M. L. (2003). Comparing social feminism and liberal feminism: The case of new firm growth. In *New perspectives on women entrepreneurs* (pp. 25–50). Information Age Publishing.

De Medeiros, J. F., Ribeiro, J. L. D., & Cortimiglia, M. N. (2014). Success factors for environmentally sustainable product innovation: A systematic literature review. *Journal of Cleaner Production, 65*, 76–86. https://doi.org/10.1016/j.jclepro.2013.08.035

Defrancesco, E., Gatto, P., & Mozzato, D. (2018). To leave or not to leave? Understanding determinants of farmers' choices to remain in or abandon agri-environmental schemes. *Land Use Policy, 76*, 460–470. https://doi.org/10.1016/j.landusepol.2018.02.026

Dessein, J., Bock, B. B., & De Krom, M. P. (2013). Investigating the limits of multifunctional agriculture as the dominant frame for Green Care in agriculture in Flanders and the Netherlands. *Journal of Rural Studies, 32*, 50–59. https://doi.org/10.1016/j.jrurstud.2013.04.011

EIP-AGRI. (2016). *EIP-AGRI Focus Group—New entrants into farming: Lessons to foster innovation and entrepreneurship*. Final Report. EIP-AGRI.

Ellis, F. (2000). *Rural livelihoods and diversity in developing countries*. Oxford University Press.

Esmaeilian, B., Sarkis, J., Lewis, K., & Behdad, S. (2020). Blockchain for the future of sustainable supply chain management in Industry 4.0. *Resources, Conservation and Recycling, 163*, 105064. https://doi.org/10.1016/j.resconrec.2020.105064

European Commission. (2019). *Communication on The European Green Deal*. https://commission.europa.eu/document/daef3e5c-a456-4fbb-a067-8f1cbe8d9c78_en

European Commission. (2021a). *Long-term vision for rural areas: For stronger, connected, resilient, prosperous EU rural areas.* https://ec.europa.eu/commission/presscorner/detail/en/ip_21_3162

European Commission. (2021b). *Digital agenda for Europe.* https://www.europarl.europa.eu/factsheets/en/sheet/64/digital-agenda-for-europe

European Commission. (2021c). *Communication from the Commission to the European Parliament, the Council, the European Economic and Social Committee and the Committee of the Regions. 2030 Digital Compass: The European way for the Digital Decade.* https://eur-lex.europa.eu/legal-content/en/TXT/?uri=CELEX%3A52021DC0118

European Commission. (2023). *'The Digitalisation of the European Agricultural Sector', 2023.* https://digital-strategy.ec.europa.eu/en/policies/digitalisation-agriculture.

European Union. (2018). *EU youth strategy.* https://youth.europa.eu/strategy_en

European Union. (2021). *EU rural development policy. Impact, challenges and outlook.* European Parliament. http://www.europarl.europa.eu/thinktank

Farrugia, D. (2016). The mobility imperative for rural youth: The structural, symbolic and non-representational dimensions of rural youth mobilities. *Journal of Youth Studies, 19*(6), 836–851. https://doi.org/10.1080/13676261.2015.1112886

Gnamus, A. (2021). *Sustainable smart specialisation strategies (S4) as the enables of co-creation of innovative green circular solution, panel discussion: Towards the green and circular economy.* 6th Forum of the EU Strategy for the Adriatic and Ionian Region, along the coasts of the shared sea, Izola, Slovenia. https://www.adriatic-ionian.eu/wp-content/uploads/2021/05/T_14_30_Towards_Ale%C5%A1-Gnamu%C5%A1.pdf

Hassink, J., Hulsink, W., & Grin, J. (2016). Entrepreneurship in agriculture and healthcare: Different entry strategies of care farmers. *Journal of Rural Studies, 43*, 27–39. https://doi.org/10.1016/j.jrurstud.2015.11.013

Hekkert, M. P., Suurs, R. A., Negro, S. O., Kuhlmann, S., & Smits, R. E. (2007). Functions of innovation systems: A new approach for analysing technological change. *Technological Forecasting and Social Change, 74*(4), 413–432. https://doi.org/10.1016/j.techfore.2006.03.002

Holloway, L., & Kneafsey, M. (2000). Reading the space of the framers' market: A case study from the United Kingdom. *Sociologia Ruralis, 40*(3), 285–299. https://doi.org/10.1111/1467-9523.00149

IFAD. (2019). *2019 Rural Development report: Creating opportunities for rural youth.*

Jean-Philippe, S., Richards, J., Gwinn, K., & Beyl, C. (2017). Urban youth perceptions of agriculture. *Journal of Youth Development, 12*(3), 1–17. https://doi.org/10.5195/jyd.2017.497

Kneafsey, M., Venn, L., Schmutz, U., Balázs, B., Trenchard, L., Eyden-Wood, T., et al. (2013). Short food supply chains and local food systems in the EU. A state of play of their socioeconomic characteristics. *JRC Scientific and Policy Reports, 123*, 129.

Knickel, K., & Renting, H. (2000). Methodological and conceptual issues in the study of multifunctionality and rural development. *Sociologia Ruralis, 40*(4), 512–528. https://doi.org/10.1111/1467-9523.00164

Laforge, J. M., & Levkoe, C. Z. (2018). Seeding agroecology through new farmer training in Canada: Knowledge, practice, and relational identities. *Local Environment, 23*(10), 991–1007. https://doi.org/10.1080/13549839.2018.1515901

Lai, J., & Widmar, N. O. (2021). Revisiting the digital divide in the COVID-19 era. *Applied Economic Perspectives and Policy, 43*(1), 458–464. https://doi.org/10.1002/aepp.13104

Li, Y., Westlund, H., & Liu, Y. (2019). Why some rural areas decline while some others not: An overview of rural evolution in the world. *Journal of Rural Studies, 68*, 135–143. https://doi.org/10.1016/j.jrurstud.2019.03.003

Manolova, T. S., Carter, N. M., Manev, I. M., & Gyoshev, B. S. (2007). The differential effect of men and women entrepreneurs' human capital and networking on growth expectancies in Bulgaria. *Entrepreneurship Theory and Practice, 31*(3), 407–426. https://doi.org/10.1111/j.1540-6520.2007.00180.x

McGreevy, S. R., Kobayashi, M., & Tanaka, K. (2019). Agrarian pathways for the next generation of Japanese farmers. *Canadian Journal of Development Studies/Revue Canadienne d'Études du Développement, 40*(2), 272–290. https://doi.org/10.1080/02255189.2018.1517642

Mujčinović, A. (2020). *Impact of public policies on quality of business of medicinal and aromatic plant producers in Bosnia and Herzegovina*, Doctoral thesis, University of Sarajevo, Faculty of Agriculture and Food Science, Sarajevo, Bosnia and Herzegovina.

Mujčinović, A., & Bojnec, Š. (2023). *Rural NEETs and sustainability – diverse, multisectoral, and multifunctional environments shaping rural areas and daily life*. COST Action CA 18213: Rural NEET Youth Network: Modeling the risks underlying rural NEETs social exclusion. ISBN: 978-989-781-755-7.

Nikolić, A., Mujčinović, A., & Bošković, D. (2022a). Get ready for Industry 4.0 – tool to support food value chain transformation. In M. Brka et al. (Eds.), *10th Central European Congress on Food* (pp. 453–476). Springer International. https://doi.org/10.1007/978-3-031-04797-8_39

Nikolić, A., Uzunović, M., & Mujčinović, A. (2022b). Perspectives and limitations of urban agriculture in transition economies: A case study in Bosnia and Herzegovina. In W. Leal Filho, I. Djekic, S. Smetana, & M. Kovaleva (Eds.), *Handbook of climate change across the food supply chain. Climate change management*. Springer. https://doi.org/10.1007/978-3-030-87934-1_4

Padel, S. (2001). Conversion to organic farming: A typical example of the diffusion of an innovation? *Sociologia Ruralis, 41*(1), 40–61. https://doi.org/10.1111/1467-9523.00169

Philip, L., & Williams, F. (2019). Remote rural home based businesses and digital inequalities: Understanding needs and expectations in a digitally underserved community. *Journal of Rural Studies, 68*, 306–318. https://doi.org/10.1016/j.jrurstud.2018.09.011

Ray, C. (2001). Transnational co-operation between rural areas: Elements of a political economy of EU rural development. *Sociologia Ruralis, 41*(3), 279–295. https://doi.org/10.1111/1467-9523.00183

Reimer, A., Thompson, A., Prokopy, L. S., Arbuckle, J. G., Genskow, K., Jackson-Smith, D., et al. (2014). People, place, behavior, and context: A research agenda for expanding our understanding of what motivates farmers' conservation behaviors. *Journal of Soil and Water Conservation, 69*(2), 57A–61A. https://doi.org/10.2489/jswc.69.2.57A

Renting, H., Oostindie, H., Laurent, C., Brunori, G., Barjolle, D., Jervell, A., et al. (2008). Multifunctionality of agricultural activities, changing rural identities and new institutional arrangements. *International Journal of Agricultural Resources, Governance and Ecology, 7*(4-5), 361–385. https://doi.org/10.1504/IJARGE.2008.020083

Riley, M. (2016). How does longer term participation in agri-environment schemes [re] shape farmers' environmental dispositions and identities? *Land Use Policy, 52*, 62–75. https://doi.org/10.1016/j.landusepol.2015.12.010

Roberts, E., Beel, D., Philip, L., & Townsend, L. (2017). Rural resilience in a digital society. *Journal of Rural Studies, 54*, 355–359. https://doi.org/10.1016/j.jrurstud.2017.06.010

Ruvio, A. A., & Shoham, A. (2011). A multilevel study of nascent social ventures. *International Small Business Journal, 29*(5), 562–579. https://doi.org/10.1177/0266242610369741

Salazar, C., Jaime, M., Pinto, C., & Acuña, A. (2019). Interaction between crop insurance and technology adoption decisions: The case of wheat farmers in Chile. *Australian Journal of Agricultural and Resource Economics, 63*(3), 593–619. https://doi.org/10.1111/1467-8489.12307

Schmidt, C., Goetz, S. J., & Tian, Z. (2021). Female farmers in the United States: Research needs and policy questions. *Food Policy, 101*, 102039. https://doi.org/10.1016/j.foodpol.2021.102039

Sestino, A., Prete, M. I., Piper, L., & Guido, G. (2020). Internet of Things and Big Data as enablers for business digitalization strategies. *Technovation, 98*, 102173. https://doi.org/10.1016/j.technovation.2020.102173

Seuneke, P., Lans, T., & Wiskerke, J. S. (2013). Moving beyond entrepreneurial skills: Key factors driving entrepreneurial learning in multifunctional agriculture. *Journal of Rural Studies, 32*, 208–219. https://doi.org/10.1016/j.jrurstud.2013.06.001

Shortall, S. (2015). Gender mainstreaming and the common agricultural policy. *Gender, Place & Culture, 22*(5), 717–730. https://doi.org/10.1080/0966369X.2014.939147

Simões, F. (2018). How to involve rural NEET youths in agriculture? Highlights of an untold story. *Community Development, 49*(5), 556–573. https://doi.org/10.1080/15575330.2018.1531899

Simões, F., Fernandes-Jesus, M., Marta, E., Albanesi, C., & Carr, N. (2023). The increasing relevance of European rural young people in policy agendas: Contributions from community psychology. *Journal of Community and Applied Social Psychology, 33*(1), 3–13. https://doi.org/10.1002/casp.2640

Simões, F., & do Rio, N. B. (2020). How to increase rural NEETs professional involvement in agriculture? The roles of youth representations and vocational training packages improvement. *Journal of Rural Studies, 75*, 9–19. https://doi.org/10.1016/j.jrurstud.2020.02.007

Simões, F., Unay-Gailhard, I., Mujčinović, A., & Fernandes, B. (2021). How to foster rural sustainability through farming workforce rejuvenation? Looking into involuntary newcomers' spatial (im) mobilities. *Sustainability, 13*(15), 8517. https://doi.org/10.3390/su13158517

Swetnam, R. D., Mountford, J. O., Manchester, S. J., & Broughton, R. K. (2004). Agri-environmental schemes: Their role in reversing floral decline in the Brue floodplain, Somerset, UK. *Journal of environmental management, 71*(1), 79–93. https://doi.org/10.1016/j.jenvman.2004.01.006

Ufuk, H., & Özgen, Ö. (2001). Interaction between the business and family lives of women entrepreneurs in Turkey. *Journal of Business Ethics, 31*, 95–106. https://doi.org/10.1023/A:1010712023858

Unay-Gailhard, İ., & Bojnec, Š. (2019). The impact of green economy measures on rural employment: Green jobs in farms. *Journal of Cleaner Production, 208*, 541–551. https://doi.org/10.1016/j.jclepro.2018.10.160

United Nations General Assembly. (1987). Report of the World Commission on Environment and Development: Our common future. Transmitted to the General Assembly as an Annex to Document A/42/427 – Development and International Co-operation: Environment.

Van der Ploeg, J. D., Renting, H., Brunori, G., Knickel, K., Mannion, J., Marsden, T., et al. (2000). Rural development: From practices and policies towards theory. *Sociologia ruralis, 40*(4), 391–408. https://doi.org/10.1111/1467-9523.00156

Verheul, I., Stel, A. V., & Thurik, R. (2006). Explaining female and male entrepreneurship at the country level. *Entrepreneurship and Regional Development, 18*(2), 151–183. https://doi.org/10.1080/08985620500532053

Walker, B. H., & Pearson, L. (2007). A resilience perspective of the SEEA. *Ecological Economics, 61*(4), 708–715. https://doi.org/10.1016/j.ecolecon.2006.04.010

Zareiyan, B., & Korjani, M. (2018). Blockchain technology for global decentralized manufacturing: Challenges and solutions for supply chain in fourth industrial revolution. *International Journal of Advanced Robotic Automation, 3*(2), 1–10. https://doi.org/10.15226/2473-3032/3/2/00135

Open Access This chapter is licensed under the terms of the Creative Commons Attribution 4.0 International License (http://creativecommons.org/licenses/by/4.0/), which permits use, sharing, adaptation, distribution and reproduction in any medium or format, as long as you give appropriate credit to the original author(s) and the source, provide a link to the Creative Commons license and indicate if changes were made.

The images or other third party material in this chapter are included in the chapter's Creative Commons license, unless indicated otherwise in a credit line to the material. If material is not included in the chapter's Creative Commons license and your intended use is not permitted by statutory regulation or exceeds the permitted use, you will need to obtain permission directly from the copyright holder.

Chapter 6
A More Youth-Centered Policy Development Perspective in NEET Policies

Emre Erdoğan and Heidi Paabort

Abstract Understanding young people's needs from their own perspective is important for effective policy making. The Youth Guarantee (YG) has been successful in providing training, job search assistance, monitoring, and public work programs for vulnerable young people (NEETs). However, the YG primarily focuses on economic aspects, ignoring multidimensional social problems faced by this vulnerable group. Our chapter focuses on the factors behind the need and on the potential of young people's contribution to policy-making making it more youth-centered. Recent academic discussions have focused on improving policy development processes beyond the classic or rationalist approach, incorporating cognitive biases, power factors, the multiplicity of actors, and the importance of the environment. To address these challenges, we present the results of a multi-country thought experiment that revealed that the national government is the most important actor in policy development for NEETs, followed by public employment services, local government, civil society organizations, and regional governments. Subsequently, we explore the potential benefits for policy development of new design thinking approaches based on the case example of the Reinforced YG of Estonia. The Estonian approach aims to address the multidimensionality of social problems faced by vulnerable young people and to promote a design-based policy development mindset, creating new avenues for support and services.

Keywords Co-creation · Design thinking · Youth-centered · Human-centered · Design-based policy · Indicators · NEET · Stakeholders

---

Author Heidi Paabort was a participant and observer in the co-creation process of the Estonian example cited in the article.

E. Erdoğan (✉)
Istanbul Bilgi University, Istanbul, Turkey
e-mail: emre.erdogan@bilgi.edu.tr

H. Paabort
Social Insurance Board, University of Tartu, Tartu, Estonia

© The Author(s) 2024
F. Simões, E. Erdogan (eds.), *NEETs in European rural areas*, SpringerBriefs in Sociology, https://doi.org/10.1007/978-3-031-45679-4_6

6.1 Introduction

Young people not in Employment, nor in Education, or Training (NEET) is a label referring to those aged 15–29 who are not enrolled in formal education or work (Mascherini et al., 2012). NEETs are increasingly at the center of academic and policy-making debates aiming at the development of national policies for responding to young people's complex solution needs. According to Eurostat (2020), the number of NEETs is on a downward trend, but the NEET rate is still higher than the European average in ten Member States (e.g., Italy, Greece). While the situation is slowly stabilizing, several research studies related to the target group (e.g., Kusa & Jasiak, 2020) have nevertheless highlighted that supporting young people's ever-evolving needs still requires several actions in different areas. The European Commission (2021) set out guidelines for Member States to achieve higher employability, better skills, stronger social protection systems, and a near-term target to reduce the share of young people in NEETs from 12.6% in 2019 to 9% in 2030. In line with this, the European Commission encouraged Member States to implement a new, strengthened Youth Guarantee (YG) with the funding of the European Union where young people under the age of 30 to support young people to find quality jobs, improve their education, or have access to an apprenticeship or a traineeship within 4 months of leaving school or becoming unemployed (European Commission, 2020).

YG interventions have reached young people mostly in countries that have developed partnerships between the public and the private sectors, including social enterprises and civil society institutions (Erdogan et al., 2021; Stabingis, 2020; Zhartay et al., 2020). Effective interventions have considered the different needs of young people when supporting them as a whole, and solutions have focused on improving the overall well-being of the young person, provided in a caring environment (Jonsson et al., 2022; Poštrak et al., 2020; Simmons, 2017). Amongst them, it is considered that the more vulnerable NEETs are likely to require longer-term and more holistic interventions to avoid the disproportionate negative impacts of risks that threaten this demographic group (European Commission, 2020). However, due to NEETs increasing vulnerabilities, policy-making has become more complex (Hooghe & Marks, 2013), translating into the need to support young people across sectors (Gaspani, 2019) and calling for coordination between many service providers (Carcillo & Königs, 2015; Mascherini, 2019). Policy agreements are seen as a solution to address these issues in a more structured way (O'Reilly et al., 2018). The YG has been successful in countries that have implemented comprehensive and well-funded programs providing young people with training, job search assistance, monitoring, subsidized employment, and public work programs.

One significant criticism made to the YG is, however, that it emphasizes mainly the economic aspects associated with NEETs, with most of the indicators developed to track this element such as the NEET or youth unemployment rates (European Commission, 2017). Although low economic security issues may be a significant consequence of becoming and staying in the NEET condition, there are additional individual and societal effects associated with this phenomenon, including social exclusion, marginalization, lack of trust in political institutions, lack of social capital, and political participation, as well as mental and physical health outcomes (Caroleo et al., 2020; Quintano et al., 2018) which merit being addressed in the YG context. Focusing on the economic outcomes may be a result of the framing and labeling of NEETs and consequently as a kind of deviation from the normal transition of life of young people. The new period of Youth Guarantee has now opened up to build on lessons learned, such as the fact that there is no longer a match between young people's needs for solutions and the opportunities created through interventions. The European Commission through the Knowledge Hub's good practices offers opportunities to create many new untapped channels to better understand vulnerable youth (Santos-Brien, 2018). An analysis of the good practices from Member States found through the Knowledge Hubs allows us to see that the majority of interventions are both coordinated and funded in a rather top-down way. At the same time, according to Butkeviciene (2009), 'bottom-up' approaches are more effective than 'top-down' initiatives because they consider local problems and involve local stakeholders. These pieces of evidence are also supported by the emergence of a new public governance approach in the public sector, where, according to Lepik and Kangro (2020), the focus is on creating shared (including societal) value through action rather than on public good and choice. Based on Poštrak et al. (2020), understanding young people's well-being and needs from their own perspective and involving them in addressing their own needs is important for effective policy making. Paabort et al. (2023) add to this, by emphasizing that there is currently not enough scientific production on what young people in the target group themselves think about youth involvement in policy-making.

In a nutshell, we find that the economy-based approach to NEETs in terms of policy development may be too narrow because it ignores the multidimensionality of social problems lived by this group of vulnerable young people. In other words, and based on the foregoing knowledge, our aim is to address the need to understand the different factors that contribute to the challenges of policy-making in relation to young people in the NEET condition, with a particular focus on strengths approach whereby the potential of young people themselves is also considered a central piece of policymaking. To achieve our aim, we are proposing to combine a new method based on the design thinking approach with the experience of development of the Reinforced Youth Guarantee of Estonia which employs the codesign approach.

We will first start by presenting the basic assumptions of the "Rationalist" policy development approach which dominated the policymaking arena for many years. We will also show that these assumptions are largely unrealistic leading to a hyperrationality of the relevant actors in policy development with every deviation from policies being explained by the irrationality of actors. Afterward, we will show the multiplicity of the relevant stakeholders and multidimensionality of priorities in policy development for NEETs, based on a survey conducted with the participation of the COST Action Rural NEET Youth Network, conducted by it Working Group 5, which is dedicated to scientific coordination. Then, we propose a method for new policy development for NEETs which is based on the design thinking approach as an alternative to the failure of the classical approach for addressing the multiple challenges faced by this group of vulnerable young people. Finally, we make an in-depth exploration of the Estonian Reinforced Youth Guarantee program as it constitutes a good starting point to understand how a design based policy development mindset may be helpful to overcome NEETs challenges.

6.2 "Rationalist" Project of Policy Development

The rationalist paradigm of policy development started in the early 1930s when rationalization meant bringing scientific knowledge and expertise to the state administration. The rationalist approach (from now on referred to as the classical model) started several analytical techniques such as cost-benefit analysis, operations and systems research, and linear programming. The major skill for policy developers was not possessing detailed knowledge about the topic; they were experts in making analyses by using "scientific methods" (Radin, 2019).

One major challenge for the rationalization of policy development was the difficulty of picking one of several possible solutions to a given problem. For the classical approach, developing alternative policies and using a filter of political and economic feasibility is one of the earlier steps of policy development. The first important dimension of the rationalist perspective was technical feasibility corresponding to the capability to implement the solution, while the second main dimension of this approach was political feasibility, referring to the willingness of the political actor to use this policy which was included in the equation (Meltsner, 1972). Policy analysts' function was to evaluate policy alternatives regarding desired and largely economic goals by using engineering techniques such as the Cost Benefit Analysis, which quantifies costs and relates them to outputs (Cairney, 2021; Dunn, 2017).

As efficiency is accepted as the major economic criterion by the classical model, recent discussions led to the enlargement of the requirements by including intangible and non-economic criteria such as adequacy, equity, responsiveness, and appropriateness (Dunn, 2017). For example, Bardach and Patashnik (2019) list "equality, equity, fairness, justice" and "freedom, community, and other ideas" as other examples of such criteria. There are some newly developed methods to address the incapacity of the classical approach to properly integrate intangible and non-economic criteria in policy development, such as considering optimizing multiple criteria or satisfying multiple goals. Multiple Criteria Analysis is described as "defining the criteria that emerge from the cost, effectiveness, political feasibility, and implementation capability categories and use them to systematically examine each alternative," combining economic goals and the feasibility criteria. Alternative policies are weighted using these criteria—the client and the analyst develop weights—and the best one has been chosen (Radin, 2019).

Even when incorporating new criteria and methods, the classical approach remains limited, and its ambition to impose rationality on policies by excluding political preferences is unrealistic, particularly when dealing with complex social situations or groups such as NEETs. Hence, the role of politics must be considered in the processes of policy development in two dimensions. First, the definition of the problem is political because problems do not exist by themselves: society constructs them (Cairney, 2021). All problems are related to the societal structure to a degree, but also, they become "social" when they attract public attention. In the public sphere, there is a kind of competition between different "problems," and sometimes, because of moral panic, some problems attract the attention of society, relevant actors, and policymakers (Clarke & Cochrane, 1998; Goode & Ben-Yehuda, 1994; Hilgartner & Bosk, 1988). Secondly, policymakers, in general, cannot be objective as have their values, priorities, and ideological preferences. Stone (1997), for instance, proposes that this approach ignores the emotions of actors. Hence, the problem detection phase is highly subjective and dependent on contextual factors such as analysts' values and political views while feasibility depends on policymakers' political and ideological preferences, due to their rather limited political agendas driven by ideological, institutional, and cognitive barriers (Baumgartner & Jones, 2010).

Another major limitation of the rationalist approach to policy development stems precisely from ignoring politics in the evaluation phase. Stone (1997) states that all criteria, including economic ones, are political. The definition of efficiency is highly dependent on questions about who determines the main goal, who benefits from different goals, and how to define resources to balance decision-making. Meanwhile, the equity criterion is related to the definition of which groups must be included but choosing a method to evaluate alternative policies is highly politically motivated (Cairney, 2021; Weimer & Vining, 2017).

Below, Table 6.1 presents different roadmaps of policy development, starting from the definition of the problem to making a decision and making recommendations. Different authors adopted the basic five-step policy development approach to respond to criticisms of hyper-rationalization.

The classical or rationalist approach has been at the center of the development of the NEET concept and of policy development in this domain. From the beginning, the objective of the policy action was to identify, within the framework of the European Employment Strategy, the group of non-employed young people who were not developing actions to improve their human capital (Serracant, 2014). This definition as a concept attracted different criticisms. To begin with, the concept seems to exclude heterogeneity of this group. There are, indeed, different typologies of NEET, thus a single definition of the target group restricts the effectiveness of policies (Furlong, 2006; Mascherini, 2019; Paabort et al., 2023). Secondly, reducing the NEET notion to an individual trait is problematic because it refers to "people than situations," ignoring structural factors such as inequalities or social policies (Brown, 2017; Holte, 2018; Serracant, 2014; Thompson, 2011). Consequently, policy development in different contexts led to the stigmatization of NEETs as lacking motivation and skills (Cabases Pique et al., 2016; Strecker et al., 2021); or as being "risky" economic subjects (McPherson, 2021). All this adds to evidence coming out from some studies showing how different discourses dominate the development of youth

Table 6.1 Comparison of different roadmaps (adapted from Cairney, 2021)

	Bardach and Patashnik (2019) A Practical Guide for Policy Analysis	Dunn (2017) Public Policy Analysis	Meltzer and Schwartz (2019) Policy Analysis as Problem-Solving	Mintrom (2011) Contemporary Policy Analysis	Weimer and Vining (2017) Policy Analysis: Concepts and Practice
1	Define the problem	What is the policy problem to be solved?	Define the problem	Engage in problem definition.	Write to Your Client
2	Assemble some evidence	What effect will each potential policy solution have?	Identify potential policy options (alternatives)	Propose alternative responses to the problem	Understand the Policy Problem
3	Construct alternatives	Which solutions should we choose, and why?	Specify the objectives to be attained in addressing the problem and the criteria to evaluate	Choose criteria for evaluating each alternative policy response	Be Explicit About Values (and goals)
4	Select the criteria	What were the policy outcomes?	Assess the outcomes of the policy options in light of the criteria and weigh trade-offs	Project the outcomes of pursuing each policy alternative.	Specify Concrete Policy Alternatives
5	Project the outcomes	Identify and analyse trade-offs among alternatives	Arrive at a recommendation	Identify and analyse trade-offs among alternatives	Predict and Value Impacts
6	Confront the trade-offs	Report findings and make an argument for the most appropriate response		Identify and analyse trade-offs among alternatives	Consider the Trade-Offs
7	Decide				Make a Recommendation
8	Tell your story				

policies such as the lack of young people's participation in economic activities or immaturity of youth, in the case of Finland (Mertanen et al., 2020) and victimization of youth in the case of Sweden (Jonsson et al., 2022).

6.3 Content and Priorities of the Relevant Stakeholders

To deliver more effective policymaking models, it is crucial to understand the various stakeholders working with or making research on NEETs. This goal can be facilitated by mapping the actors supporting young people in the NEET condition. However, this is a complex task as it requires the participation of multiple actors involved with the target group. Additionally, it is challenging to create a global stakeholder map with active agents and their priorities, since every social problem has local, national, and global components. Nonetheless, a multi-country thought experiment could help us comprehend the policymaking landscape, key actors, and policy agendas.

To address this challenge, we surveyed the members of the COST Action Rural NEET Youth Network on issues related to policies for NEETs. We asked them to list relevant policy actors and their priorities related to policies addressing this group of vulnerable young people. Forty-two members representing 19 countries answered the questionnaire. Below we summarise the survey results, which formed the basis of the stakeholder mapping exercise.

According to Table 6.2, the major actor in the policy development towards NEETs is the national government: 36 out of 42 participants put the government among the five most important actors. The national government is followed by public employment services (31) and the local government (26). More than half of the participants stated civil society organizations (24), and for 17 participants, regional governments are the most important actors in policy development. Development agencies and business organizations are not among the most frequently stated actors. An important point here is that only two participants state labor unions. Since the NEET problem has generally been perceived as a labor market problem, such an exclusion shows the limitations of the existing policy development perspective. Other actors listed by the participants are educational institutions and agricultural development cooperatives. Another interesting finding is that only two participants listed youth organizations—The National Youth Council and The Agency for Youth and Sport—another indicator of exclusion of the most important stakeholder of the problem, the youth sector. These findings show that policy

Table 6.2 Most frequently stated actors in NEET policy development

Actors in NEET policy development	n
National government	36
Public Employment Services	31
Local government	26
Civil society organizations	24
Regional government(s)	17
Other	7
Development Agencies	6
Business organizations	6
Labor unions	2
European Employment Agency	1

Table 6.3 Most frequently stated objectives in NEET policy development

Objectives in NEET policy development	n
Creating employment	79
Improving skills	78
Facilitating school-job transition	60
Reducing inequalities	58
Stimulating economic growth	43
Stimulating competitiveness	33
Facilitate the match between labour demand and labour supply	16
Economically support people during their job search process	14

development is highly centralized in participating countries, giving extraordinary power to national governments and national employment agencies. The role assigned to local and regional governments may be accounted for attempts for localization of solutions. Meanwhile, the lack of labor unions and youth associations must be analyzed in detail.

We also asked participants to pick the major motivations of these actors from a list of nine policy objectives. These results are presented in Table 6.3.

Our results show that the most important policy motivation is creating employment followed by improving skills. Facilitating school-job transition and reducing inequalities are two other leading motivations. Stimulation of economic growth and competitiveness are among the frequently stated motivations. However, providing economic support to youth during their job search process and facilitating the match between labor demand and supply are relatively less frequently mentioned motivations. Thus, economic priorities are the leading motivations of policies targeting NEETs according to our survey.

The correspondence map that is presented in Fig. 6.1 adds to our discussion by intersecting the leading policy actors with their motivations for developing policies targeting NEETs. Correspondence analysis is an analytical technique for displaying the relationship between two variables, in our case actors and their motivations. Motivations located closer to actors show that these participants more frequently stated these motivations compared to other actors and motivations. If an actor or motivation is located closer to the center of the map, it shows an agreement on these issues (Greenacre, 2010).

According to the above figure, stimulating competitiveness and economically supporting people are perceived as the main motivations of national and local governments. Similarly, stimulating economic growth is closer to national and local governments. On the lower right quadrant of the map, we observe that reducing inequalities is close to development agencies and civil society organizations. It is also possible to state that reducing inequalities and economically supporting people are relatively closer to the local government, meaning that these distributional goals are assigned to the local authorities such as local governments and development agencies.

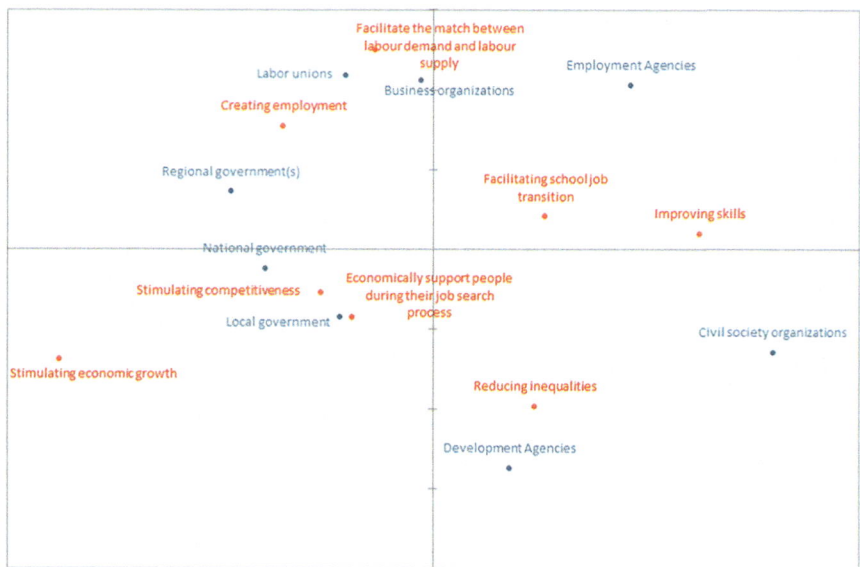

Fig. 6.1 Correspondence map intersecting actors and their motivations

On the top of the correspondence map, we observe that labor market-related motivations are closer to the economic actors. Facilitating the match between labor demand and labor supply is perceived as closer to labor unions, business organizations, and employment agencies. Labor unions, business organizations, and regional governments are closer to creating employment motivation. Facilitating school-job transitions and improving skills are closer to civil society organizations and employment agencies.

In sum, the correspondence map shows us how motivations for policies are diversified; different levels of government—national, regional, and local governments—are perceived as being motivated by stimulating economic growth and competitiveness and creating employment. The social dimensions of the NEET condition are related to local actors, development agencies, and civil society organizations.

Figure 6.2 presents a network analysis of actors and motivations. It is a bipartite network map combining two different layers, actors, and their motivations. Indeed, social network analysis allows us to understand any field not by only focusing on the relative positioning of actors and policies; additionally, it also considers the relationship between actors, objectives, actors, and objectives (Wasserman & Faust, 1994).

Similar to Fig. 6.1, the network map shown in Fig. 6.2 illustrates the central role of the national government on the map. This agency is connected to almost every policy, especially stimulating economic growth, facilitating school-job transition, and facilitating the match between labor demand and labor supply. Moreover, the national government is motivated to support people during their job search process

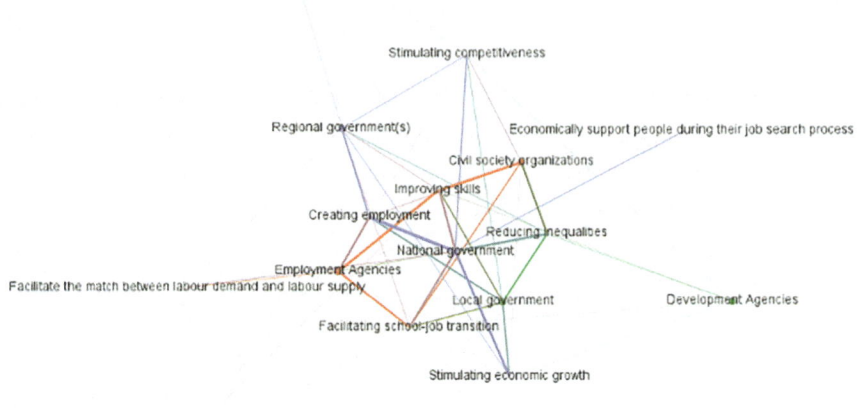

Fig. 6.2 Cocitation network map of actors and motivations

and reduce inequalities. Another centrally located actor is the local government, which seems to be connected with reducing inequalities together with development agencies; facilitating school-job transition and the match between demand and supply in the labor market and employment agencies. Public employment services are close to creating employment and facilitating the match between labor demand and labor supply. Labor unions are close to these public agencies in the network map. Together with regional governments, employment agencies are closely related to the motivation of creating employment. Improving skills, stimulating competitiveness, and economically supporting people are motivations of civil society organizations. Business organizations are located on the top of the network map and are mainly motivated by stimulating competitiveness. Thus, the network map of actors and motivations further supports our argument about the centrality of the national government, while confirming the marginalized roles of labor unions and business organizations. Moreover, this map also demonstrates that distributional policies are in the domain of the local government and civil society organizations.

As the network of actors and motivations was bipartite, there is a need to analyze each network separately. Figure 6.3. illustrates separately the distribution of actors and motivations.

Figure 6.3 shows the centrality of the national government sharing the same motivations with almost every stakeholder. Local governments, employment agencies, regional governments, and civil society organizations are closely connected to this central agent. Meanwhile, business organizations, labor unions, and development agencies have peripheral roles based on their motivations.

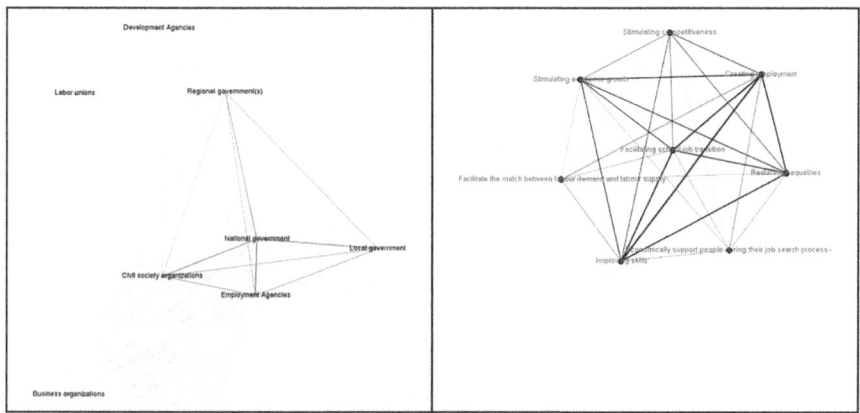

Fig. 6.3 Separate cocitation network of actors and motivations

When we focus on the motivations network, we observe that several motivations have central roles. Facilitating school-job transition, creating employment, and stimulating economic growth are keystones of the motivations' network. On the other hand, stimulating competitiveness relates to stimulating economic growth and creating employment. Reducing inequalities is closely connected with supporting people during their job search and improving skills, which may be accepted as a kind of social triad. Facilitating the match between labor demand and supply is in the same triangle as stimulating economic growth and improving skills, with a focus on the market. This figure clearly shows that the economic agendas are central to developing NEET policies, while the social consequences of being in the NEET condition are perceived as being peripheral. Similarly, economic growth and adjustment of labor demand and supply may be accepted as long-term problems.

6.4 Changing the Perspective: Potential of Co-creation and Design Thinking as a Human-Centred Approach in NEET Policy

As we have discussed in the introduction section, recent academic discussions have focused on improving the policy development process beyond the classic or rationalist approach. There are some attempts to criticize idealized processes of policy development, while making them more realistic by including the cognitive biases, the power factor, the multiplicity of actors, and the importance of the environment (Bacchi, 2009; Cairney, 2021; Radin, 2019; Stone, 1997; Sucha & Sienkiewicz, 2020).

In recent years, the dissemination of research literature on policy-making for young people in the NEET condition has been complemented by co-creation and

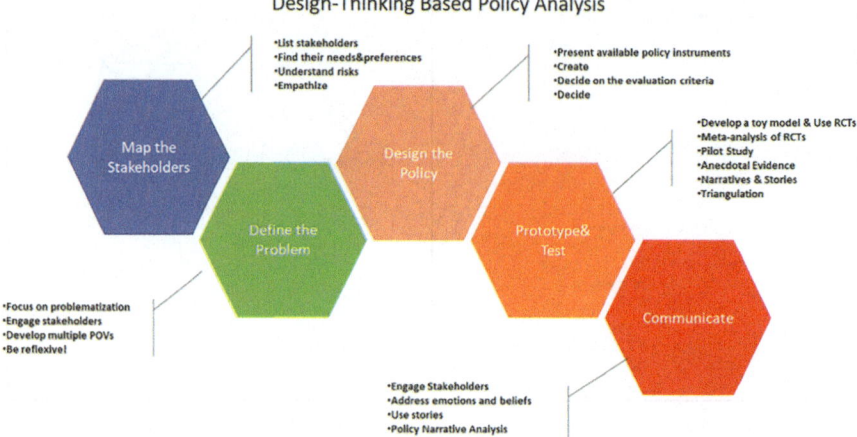

Fig. 6.4 A model of design thinking based policy analysis

design-thinking approaches. There is no standard definition of a co-creative approach based on Voorberg et al. (2013) and Windsor (2017). Still, Pedanik et al. (2021), for example, have pointed out that co-creation is a concept that encompasses all stages of service planning and delivery, considering the needs of the target group and the capabilities of service providers. In particular, it is seen as a generic concept or a needs-led design process (Voorberg et al., 2013; Windsor, 2017), where different actors work together to create agreed public services. It is essential to observe that the process results in a consensual solution, first and foremost, to develop and implement new practices. An important factor in co-creation is the continuous (further) development of the service (intervention) that is created, which, according to Osborne (2018), helps to continuously develop the service precisely in response to the needs of the client.

Design thinking is also a concept, method, or process to respond to complex design problems in the design sector. It is defined as a "human-centered approach to problem-solving". It is a discipline that uses the designer's sensibility and methods to match people's needs with what is technologically feasible. It is a non-linear process that converts social problems (Baker & Moukhliss, 2020) into opportunities and solves design problems by focusing on "what is desirable from the users' perspective, what is technically feasible, and what is commercially viable for the organization." (Kimbell, 2011:294). This approach visualizes and brings different constraints to the table during the design process. The steps in the process are presented in Fig. 6.4. Including the following tasks: (1) map the stakeholders; (2) define the problems; (3) design the policy; (4) prototype & test; and (5) communicate.

6.5 Design Thinking Approach Through the Estonian Example of Creating Policies for NEET

There is limited information in the literature on the inclusion of NEETs in policy-making using the design-thinking method or the co-creation approach (Paabort et al., 2023). One of the few known countries which adopted a co-creation and a design-thinking approach at the same time to policy development aiming at NEETs is Estonia. Therefore, we detail this case as an exemplary illustration of new policy development avenues for this group of vulnerable young people.

Co-creation and design-thinking were used as the methodological basis for the Reinforced YG Guidelines' new action line of the YG Estonia Action Plan. The plan upholds the "Implementation of a cooperation model for support and services for young people in NEET situations" for the years 2023–2029 (Paabort & Kõiv, 2022). The process of setting up the action line involved all the different actors. The state decision was based on the nationally agreed principle (Ministry of Social Affairs, 2022) that young people are the experts in their own lives, and for this reason, they know how they want to get the support they need at different stages of their personal development. The co-creation approach and the involvement of the target group resulted in several thematic studies in Estonia (e.g., Käger et al., 2020; Melesk et al., 2021). In the case of Estonia, co-creation was seen as a way of thinking underpinning the process of service creation at both the service planning and delivery stages, where different parties find the best practical solution through equal partnership, empowering each other and seeing the links between common parts of the issue. The technical implementation of the process was carried out using design thinking-based steps.

For the pilot development of this strategy of using the concept of co-creation and for implementing the process through the design-thinking approach in Estonia, a neutral party was found through a procurement process, which set up the initial process and involved all the necessary parties. The most important thing was to reach a consensus between the parties, regardless of position, to find the best way to support young people (Education and Youth Board, 2021). Below we describe how the process was developed, step by step, according to Fig. 6.4.

6.5.1 Mapping

The first step of designing a human-centred approach is to draw a field map using Stakeholder Analysis (Aligica, 2006; Dobel, 2005). This map must cover the main actors (stakeholders), including the user, their priorities, and the relationship between these actors. In the case of Estonia, in-depth document analysis—previous policies, interventions, stakeholders, and key learning experiences—was first carried out to map the context (Pedanik et al., 2021). The process included thematic meso-, macro-, and micro-level cooperation partners: ministries, umbrella associations,

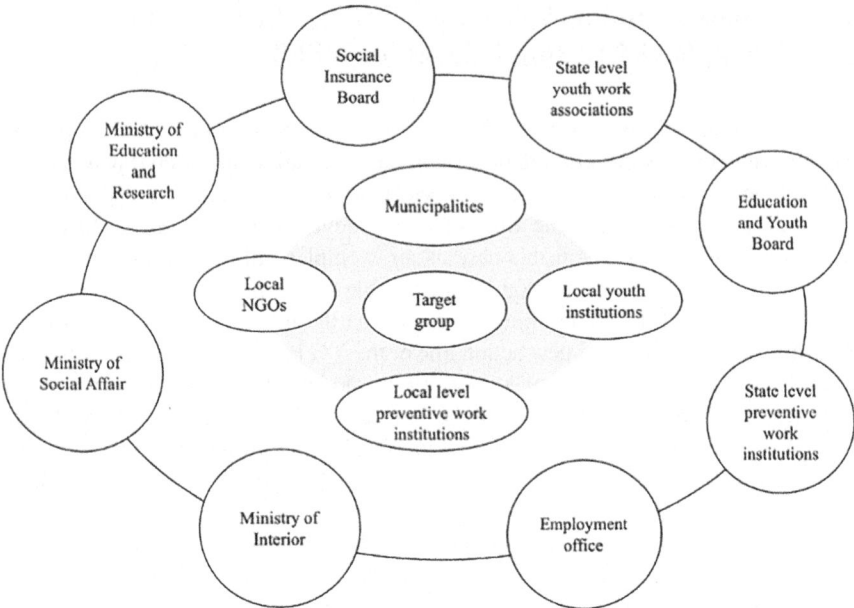

Fig. 6.5 Involved local and national stakeholders in the design process

implementers of interventions, municipalities, associations representing young people, and the target group itself (Fig. 6.5).

6.5.2 Define the Problem

The second stage of design-based political analysis involves collaboratively integrating the previous stage's findings. The classical model of political analysis leaves this initiative to the policy analysts to mitigate politicians' irrational and short-term oriented interventions. The design-based approach encourages the engagement of stakeholders in the problem definition stage. Bacchi (2009) proposes focusing on the problematization of any issue instead of accepting it as given. The problematization process will enable the policy analyst to formulate his/her own argument in the last stage. The second stage of the design process is required to understand the needs of stakeholders, not only direct beneficiaries but also policymakers and other actors. This stage will also facilitate integrating irrational elements such as cognitive biases, emotions, beliefs, and prejudices. Ethnographic methods can be used to collect the stories and narratives of the stakeholders. The problem definition stage gives the designer a Point of View (POV); in the case of policy analysis, the multiplicity of actors requires the development of multiple POVs with different priorities. This engagement must be dialogical, and empathy to understand the needs of other parties is critical.

In the case of the YG Estonia Action Plan, a series of discussions were carried out between the parties to understand the participants' perceptions, patterns, prejudices, and values about the nature of NEETs. The process carried out in Estonia included interviews and ethnographic observation of NEETs and professionals working with young people, as well as co-creative discussions between different actors supporting young people, which resulted in the development of both possible personas and persona-based solutions (Pedanik et al., 2021; Social Insurance Board, 2021), where the personas were considered to be an aggregated portrait of the client of the support activity.

Through the interviews, the young people's problems, needs, and perceived realities were mapped in depth because a more general mapping of young people's needs and expectations is important to help experts working with young people to understand how young people in NEET situations function in their daily lives and what obstacles they face. The survey results helped to complement and/or to develop services for young people in NEET situations and support them in the most appropriate way.

The ideate stage of design thinking corresponds to the classical policy analysis model's feasibility, evaluation, and prediction stages. The human-centered approach tries to bring more human factors to the policy development process, meaning all ignored factors will be considered during the design phase.

6.5.3 Design the Policy

The design thinking approach divides the step of designing the policy into two separate phases, creation and decision. In this stage, the participation of all relevant stakeholders is also critical to bring different perspectives into the creation phase, as the diversity of opinions is accepted as the best way to have viable solutions to problems. In the political domain, new policies are always linked with existing ones, so this stage must start with presenting the existing policies. Based on the multiple POVs, the team tries to develop new policies after being informed about the available policy instruments (Dam & Siang, 2019).

The design thinking approach is a process of generating as many solutions as possible without worrying about technical and political feasibility problems. It has the constraints of technical feasibility, usability, and profitability, but the action space of the product designers is larger compared to policymakers. The decision stage is more difficult than a typical product development process, as it requires the participation of all stakeholders in the design process. Different voting procedure alternatives are possible (Dam & Siang, 2019).

In the Estonian case, the third stage revealed the main problems and barriers of NEETs by delivering and exploring six personas of young people in the NEET condition. Those personas were used as input to the description of the future model (Pedanik et al., 2021). The resulting future model was validated with a co-creation process core group like ministries and implementation members. The process resulted in a two-tiered set of proposals on how to know more about, locate and support young people at risk or in a NEET situation at the local level. The proposals and guidelines in the finalized document were sent out to both municipalities and national actors to ensure a common understanding of needs and possible solutions (Pedanik et al., 2021; Social Insurance Board, 2021).

6.5.4 Prototype and Test

The next step of the design thinking approach is the prototyping phase, where designers develop small and inexpensive prototypes of the solution selected in the ideation phase and open this prototype to the user experience. It is possible to use high- and low-fidelity techniques to evaluate the outcome of the prototypical tool or intervention. High-fidelity techniques are Randomized Controlled Trials (RCTs), which are experimental forms of impact evaluation advocated by international organizations such as the World Bank or UNICEF (Gibson et al., 2017; Pearce & Raman, 2014); systematic reviews of RCTs (Oliver et al., 2008; Uman, 2011); or a pilot study limited to single geography bringing detailed quantitative and qualitative information about the desired outcomes of the policy (Gibson et al., 2017; Pearce & Raman, 2014).

Storytelling, service advertisement, video prototyping, and roleplaying among others constitute low-fidelity techniques. A storytelling approach involves experts and practitioners sharing their experiences relevant to the above-developed prototype, and testaments of the beneficiaries of similar programs may be accepted as indirect data about the performance of the policy (Cairney, 2021; Cairney & Oliver, 2017; Dam & Siang, 2019).

In the case of the Estonian example, in this phase, a survey was carried out with ten interviews and four young people with NEET status. Six experts whose daily work involves working with young people with NEET status were also interviewed. The interviews were used to validate the client journeys developed in the workshops, in order to get feedback from the young people on the journeys developed by the experts, and to incorporate the young people's views and perceptions of which current practices are not working, the reasons for this and what they think the process of accessing support should be. As a result of the survey interviews, the profiles of young people, based on the experts' experiences and knowledge, were completed and described in depth.

An important factor of co-production is the continuous co-production or (further) development of the service (intervention), which, according to Osborne (2018), contributes to the continuous development of the service, specifically in response to the needs of the client. In the Estonian case, based on the document, a final framework for a collaborative model for young people in NEETs has been developed, which will be the basis for a pilot project in 2023, where 10 local municipalities will be able to implement it in their area with the needs of the established approach (Social Insurance Board, 2021). Also, it was important to validate the results of the co-design process with institutions that were not directly involved in the process but whose work could be related to or be influenced by the guidelines of Estonian's YG. In the context of the Estonia YG, the lack of linkages between different sectoral structures and guidelines is an important limiting barrier to enabling cooperation at the local level (Paabort & Beilmann, 2021). As a result of the pilot project, an action plan for the next 5 years for NEETs and those at risk of becoming NEETs is being prepared in Estonia, which in turn will serve as a basis for the Ministry of Economic Affairs and Information Technology to direct additional resources to local authorities to ensure that changes and approaches based on the needs identified by young people receive state support in the period 2024–2029 (Social Insurance Board, 2021).

6.5.5 Communicate

The final step in classical policy-making and design thinking is the communication of results—the communication phase. If the output of the policy analysis is a policy proposal, and its implementation in real life depends on its acceptance by policymakers, then the final product of the design thinking approach is ready to be implemented in the real world after completing the team's assessment.

The classical approach leaves the responsibility of communication to the analyst. It is accepted that alternative policies in different problem domains are competing, and the policy proposal's survival depends on the quality of its communication. The engagement of the relevant stakeholders is the key element of design thinking. Hence some of the receivers are represented to a degree in the formulation of the policy proposal. For example, Cairney and Kwiatkowski (2017) propose to "Understand your audience and tailor your response" and "engage with real-world policymaking rather than waiting for a 'rational' and orderly process to appear" as two of their three steps approaches. These two proposals are already embedded in the design thinking process. Similarly, Bardach and Patashnik (2019) advice to "gauge your audience" is a task to be completed in the first phase of stakeholder mapping and empathizing.

The Estonian YG development was supported by the immediate involvement of different levels and parties in the operational phase of communication. Therefore, it was already possible to foresee risks during the process, mitigate them through joint discussions, and prepare the legal framework for the implementation of ideas.

Mainly there are suggestions to use stories in the communication stage (Davidson, 2017). Cairney and Rummery (2018) also propose communicating the results through storytelling, focusing on the emotions and beliefs of the audience using stories. Stone (1997) also describes narrative stories as the principal means for defining and contesting problems. For Rhodes (2019), the importance given to storytelling indicates the increased popularity of the "interpretive approach". Storytelling is always accepted as an important component of the design thinking process, especially during the Empathise stage and several strategies are developed to improve the effectiveness of storytelling (Elmansy, 2018; Hunsucker & Siegel, 2015).

In the Estonian example, storytelling was used in a collaborative policy document, where the personas created in the design process enabled different actors supporting young people, such as local government, the unemployment fund, youth work institutions, social services, etc. to recognize the potential of their own field and make the necessary connections from a youth support perspective. This was done from the point of view of knowing, finding, contacting, supporting, and following up young people. Thus, the linking of the six-person stories into a common case management model of support needs helped to understand what the local authority needs to be able to offer in supporting young people. As the document was created in cooperation with the national institutions responsible for the YG Estonia Action Plan, it provides a shared vision and understanding of resources through which to move forward in further cooperation. In turn, this will also allow for a harmonized understanding of how to describe and analyze the effectiveness of youth support.

Figure 6.6 summarizes the co-creation approach, national agreements, equal roles of the parties, broad awareness of good practices, and the real needs of young people in developing the Estonian YG Plan. This model of cooperation can be adapted to the context of different local authorities in Estonia and across other countries. Its implementation, with the support of public resources, will be a multi-level learning experience, which in turn will allow for continuous development of policies.

6.6 Conclusion

Our article shows that there is a need for a number of shifts in services and policy-making for NEET young people. This is even more required in a world facing a new set of problems, namely polycrises such as pandemics, climate change, inequality, polarization, and wars. These new challenges require the development of new instruments to develop better policies, putting the perspective of the subject of these policies. Our methodological approach and lessons from the Estonian experience of co-design may help us to have better instruments. First, we need to accept the fact that changing the framing of the NEET "problem" will open new avenues of policy research. Secondly, this new perspective will allow us to design better policies and develop better solutions for NEETs.

6.6.1 New Research Avenues

- **Beyond the economic approach to NEETs.** There is a need to reframe the situation of NEETs as a multidimensional problem and focus on non-economic and social consequences such as well-being, self-esteem, and confidence.

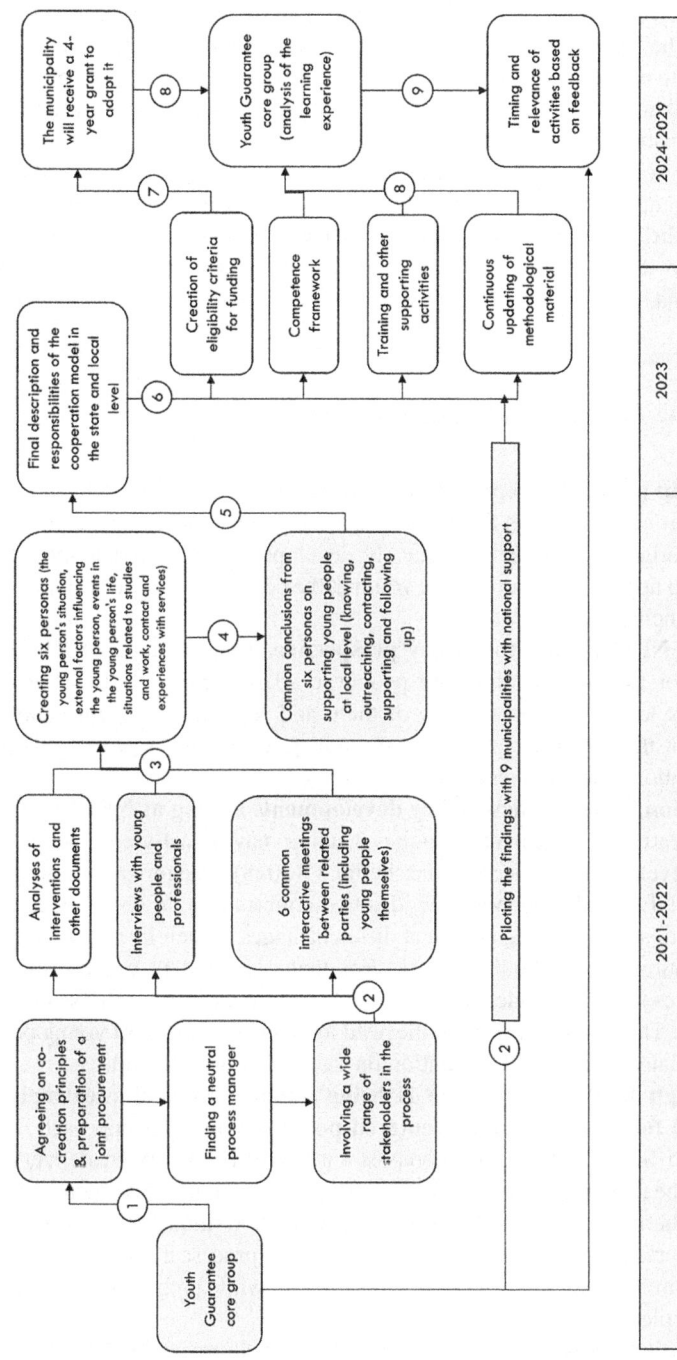

Fig. 6.6 The logic and steps of the design process of one of support measures Estonia YG Plan

- **Bring in young people's voices to research efforts.** Top-down data collection efforts such as surveys are not sufficient to understand the perspective of young people. The importance of understanding young people's differences and their reactions to established systems, allows us to better understand how young people perceive themselves in order to reduce the contradictions between young people and established systems (Görlich & Katznelson, 2018).
- **Diversify research methods.** Bringing the voice of the youth back to the policy development process, we need to rely on multimethod and multi-context research, by using different data collection methods and triangulation conducted in diverse settings to duly describe between- and within-country variation of the NEET phenomena.

6.6.2 New Policy Development Process

- **Bottom-up policy development approaches are needed.** The "classical" rationalist approach focuses on the development of effective and efficient policies and these criteria has been technocratically developed. Our approach shows that a bottom-up approach by putting the youth at the center of policy development will be more inclusive.
- **Redefine NEETs from the policy perspective.** The definition of NEETs as a problem or as a failure of young people to adapt themselves to labor market conditions leads to stigmatization of them and stigmatized young people who cannot put their own perspective to the policy development process. This conceptualization must be overcome.
- **Co-creation is key for new policy developments aiming at NEETs.** Developing co-creative environments in policy-making may attract young people to the policy development process. Mascherini's (2018) categorization of policies targeting NEETs also supports the idea that policies have to see a wider context and need to support young people at different stages of their lives, not just during the transition from school to work. For that, we need to explore their own experiences to further understand their real needs and to develop possible coping strategies. This vision is line with the need to include the voice of young people is also stipulated in the UN Convention on the Rights of the Child.
- **The design thinking approach is being adopted as an increasingly used threshold for creating people-centered policies.** While this approach may not always be linear and is more complex than traditional service delivery, as it requires the participation of all stakeholders in a design process where consensus needs to be constantly sought, it does allow for the immediate involvement of stakeholders, where already during the co-creative process it is possible to foresee risks and mitigate them through joint discussion, while preparing the legal space for the implementation of ideas.
- **Coordination is key for the success of policy development for NEETs.** A more open mindset and a more coherent cross-sectoral understanding open up the

possibility for social innovation, allowing for a better understanding of the nature of the target audience and the creation of new multidisciplinary collaborative forms expressed by young people themselves in the design process. This approach is also supported by the European Commission (2021) in its new guidelines for implementing the second period of the Youth Guarantee.

References

Aligica, P. D. (2006). Institutional and stakeholder mapping: Frameworks for policy analysis and institutional change. *Public Organization Review, 6*, 79–90. https://doi.org/10.1007/s11115-006-6833-0

Bacchi, C. (2009). *Analysing policy*. Pearson Higher Education AU.

Baker, F. W., III, & Moukhliss, S. (2020). Concretising design thinking: A content analysis of systematic and extended literature reviews on design thinking and human-centred design. *Review of Education, 8*(1), 305–333. https://doi.org/10.1002/rev3.3186

Bardach, E., & Patashnik, E. M. (2019). *A practical guide for policy analysis: The eightfold path to more effective problem solving*. CQ Press.

Baumgartner, F. R., & Jones, B. D. (2010). *Agendas and instability in American politics*. University of Chicago Press.

Brown, K. (2017). The governance of vulnerability: Regulation, support and social divisions in action. *International Journal of Sociology and Social Policy, 37*(11–12), 667–682. https://doi.org/10.1108/IJSSP-04-2016-0049

Butkeviciene, E. (2009). Social innovation in rural communities: Methodological framework and empirical evidence. *Social Sciences/Socialiniai mokslai, 1*, 80–88.

Cabases Pique, M. A., Pardell Vea, A., & Strecker, T. (2016). The EU youth guarantee—A critical analysis of its implementation in Spain. *Journal of Youth Studies, 19*(5), 684–704. https://doi.org/10.1080/13676261.2015.1098777

Cairney, P. (2021). *The politics of policy analysis*. Springer.

Cairney, P., & Kwiatkowski, R. (2017). How to communicate effectively with policymakers: Combine onsights from psychology and policy Studies. *Palgrave Communications, 3*(1), 1–8. https://doi.org/10.1057/s41599-017-0046-8

Cairney, P., & Oliver, K. (2017). Evidence-based policymaking is not like evidence-based medicine, so how far should you go to bridge the divide between evidence and policy? *Health Research Policy and Systems, 15*(1), 1–11. https://doi.org/10.1186/s12961-017-0192-x

Cairney, P., & Rummery, K. (2018). Feminising politics to close the evidence-policy gap: The case of social policy in Scotland. *Australian Journal of Public Administration, 77*(4), 542–553. https://doi.org/10.1111/1467-8500.12266

Carcillo, S., & Königs, S. (2015). *NEET youth in the aftermath of the crisis: Challenges and policies*. OECD Social, Employment and Migration Working Papers, No. 164. OECD Publishing. https://doi.org/10.2139/ssrn.2573655

Caroleo, F. E., Rocca, A., Mazzocchi, P., & Quintano, C. (2020). Being NEET in Europe before and after the economic crisis: An analysis of the micro and macro determinants. *Social Indicators Research, 149*(3), 991–1024. https://doi.org/10.1007/s11205-020-02270-6

Clarke, J., & Cochrane, A. (1998). The social construction of social problems. *Embodying the Social: Constructions of Difference*, 3–42.

Dam, R., & Siang, T. (2019). Stage 2 in the design thinking process: Define the problem and interpret the results. *Interaction Design Foundation*. https://www.interaction-design.org/literature/article/stage-2-in-the-design-thinking-process-define-the-problem-and-interpret-the-results

Davidson, B. (2017). Storytelling and evidence-based policy: Lessons from the grey literature. *Palgrave Communications, 3*(1). https://doi.org/10.1057/palcomms.2017.93

Dobel, J. P. (2005). *A note on mapping: Understanding who can influence your success*. University of Washington: Electronic Hallway. Available at SSRN: https://ssrn.com/abstract=2748329

Dunn, W. N. (2017). *Public policy analysis: An integrated approach*. Routledge.

Education and Youth Board. (2021). *Creating a future collaborative model of service design to support young people in NEET situations*.

Elmansy, D. R. (2018). *The role of storytelling in the design process*. Designorate. https://www.designorate.com/the-role-of-storytelling-in-the-design-process/.

Erdogan, E., Flynn, P., Nasya, B., Paabort, H., & Lendzhova, V. (2021). NEET rural–urban ecosystems: The pole of urban social innovation diffusion in supporting sustainable rural pathways to education, employment, and training. *Sustainability, 13*(21). https://doi.org/10.3390/su132112053

European Commission. (2017). *Data collection for monitoring of youth guarantee schemes: 2015*. https://ec.europa.eu/social/BlobServlet?docId=17426&langId=en.

European Commission. (2020). Communication from the Commission to the European Parliament, the Council, the European Economic and Social Committee.

European Commission. (2021). Council Recommendation on A Bridge to Jobs – Reinforcing the Youth Guarantee and replacing Council Recommendation of 22 April 2013 on establishing a Youth Guarantee.

Eurostat. (2020). *Young people neither in employment nor in education and training by sex, age and labour status (NEET rates)*. https://ec.europa.eu/eurostat.

Furlong, A. (2006). Not a very NEET solution: Representing problematic labour market transitions among early school-leavers. *Work Employment and Society, 20*(3), 553–569. https://doi.org/10.1177/0950017006067001

Gaspani, F. (2019). Young adults NEET and everyday life: Time management and temporal subjectivities. *Young, 27*(1), 69–88. https://doi.org/10.1177/1103308818761424

Gibson, M., Sautmann, A., Feeney, L., & Walsh, C. (2017). *Introduction to randomized evaluations. The Abdul Latif Jameel Poverty Action Lab (J-PAL)*. https://www.povertyactionlab.org/resource/introduction-randomized-evaluations?lang=fr

Goode, E., & Ben-Yehuda, N. (1994). Moral panics: Culture, politics, and social construction. *Annual Review of Sociology*, 149–171.

Görlich, A., & Katznelson, N. (2018). Young people on the margins of the educational system: Following the same path differently. *Educational Research, 60*(1), 47–61.

Greenacre, M. J. (2010). Correspondence analysis. *Wiley Interdisciplinary Reviews: Computational Statistics, 2*(5), 613–619.

Hilgartner, S., & Bosk, C. L. (1988). The rise and fall of social problems: A public arenas model. *American Journal of Sociology, 94*(1), 53–78.

Holte, B. H. (2018). Counting and meeting NEET young people: Methodology, perspective and meaning in research on marginalized youth. *Young, 26*(1), 1–16. https://doi.org/10.1177/1103308816677618

Hooghe, L., & Marks, G. (2013). Beyond federalism: Estimating and explaining the territorial structure of government. *Publius: The Journal of Federalism, 43*(2), 179–204. https://doi.org/10.1093/publius/pjs029

Hunsucker, A. J., & Siegel, M. A. (2015). Once upon a time: Storytelling in the design process. *Proceedings of the 3rd International Conference for Design Education Researchers, 1*, 443–454.

Jonsson, F., Goicolea, I., Hjelte, J., & Linander, I. (2022). Representing a fading welfare system that is failing young people in 'NEET' situations: A WPR Analysis of Swedish Youth Policies. *Journal of Applied Youth Studies, 5*(1), 75–90. https://doi.org/10.1007/s43151-022-00071-x

Käger, M., Õunapuu, T., Kivistik, K., Tambur, M., & Kaldur, K. (2020). *Analysis of the impact and effectiveness of the implementation of the Youth Guarantee Support System*. Final report. MTÜ Balti Uuringute Instituut and OÜ LevelLab. Ministry of Social Affairs.

Kimbell, L. (2011). Rethinking design thinking: Part I. *Design and Culture, 3*(3), 285–306.

Kusa, N., & Jasiak, K. (2020). An analysis of NEETs situation in UE-28 countries and the example of The Netherlands. *Przegląd Politologiczny, 3*, 39–51. https://doi.org/10.14746/pp.2020.25.3.4

Lepik, K. L., & Kangro, K. (2020). Avalike teenuste korraldamisest ja nende innovatsioonist koosloome abil [Co-creation and innovation of public services]. *Acta Politica Estica, 11*, 137–152.

Mascherini, M. (2018). *Good practices in dealing with young people who are NEETs: Policy responses at European level.* The Pontifical Academy of Social Sciences. https://www.pass.va/en/publications/acta/acta_21_pass/mascherini.html

Mascherini, M. (2019). Origins and future of the concept of NEETs in the European policy agenda. In J. O'Reilly, J. Leschke, R. Ortlieb, M. Seeleib-Kaiser, & P. Villa (Eds.), *Comparing youth transitions in Europe: Joblessness, insecurity, and inequality* (pp. 503–529). Oxford Press.

Mascherini, M., Salvatore, L., Meierkord, A., & Jungblut, J. M. (2012). *NEETs.* Publications Office of the European Union.

McPherson, C. (2021). Between the rhetoric of employability and the reality of youth (under-)employment: NEET policy rhetoric in the UK and Scotland. *Journal of Applied Youth Studies, 4*(2), 135–152. https://doi.org/10.1007/s43151-021-00045-5

Melesk, K., Koppel, K., Laurimäe, M., Nuiamäe, M., Jaanits, J., & Beilmann, K. (2021). *Evaluating the impact and effectiveness of the My First Job service.* Praxis Centre for Policy Studies.

Meltsner, A. J. (1972). Political feasibility and policy analysis. *Public Administration Review*, 859–867.

Meltzer, R., & Schwartz, A. (2019). *Policy analysis as problem solving: A flexible and evidence-based framework.* Routledge.

Mertanen, K., Pashby, K., & Brunila, K. (2020). Governing of young people 'at risk' with the alliance of employability and precariousness in the EU youth policy steering. *Policy Futures in Education, 18*(2), 240–260. https://doi.org/10.1177/14782103198386

Ministry of Social Affairs. (2022). *National Action Plan for Strengthening Youth Guarantee for the period 2022–2027.*

Mintrom, M. (2011). *Contemporary policy analysis.* Oxford University Press.

O'Reilly, J., Leschke, J., Ortlieb, R., Seeleib-Kaiser, M., & Villa, P. (2018). *Youth labor in transition: Inequalities, mobility, and policies in Europe.* Oxford University Press. https://doi.org/10.1093/oso/9780190864798.001.0001

Oliver, S., Bagnall, A., Thomas, J., Shepherd, J., Sowden, A., White, I., Dinnes, J., Rees, R., Colquitt, J., & Oliver, K. (2008). *RCTs for policy interventions. A review of reviews and meta-regression.* Centre for Reviews and Dissemination.

Osborne, P. S. (2018). From public service-dominant logic to public service logic: Are public service organizations capable of co-production and value co-creation? *Public Management Review, 20*, 225–231. https://doi.org/10.1080/14719037.2017.1350461

Paabort, H., & Beilmann, M. (2021). State level agreed-upon factors contributing more effective policymaking for public sector services for effective local-level work with NEETs. *Revista Calitatea Vieții, 32*(4).

Paabort, H., Flynn, P., Beilmann, M., & Petrescu, C. (2023). Policy responses to real world challenges associated with NEET youth: A scoping review. *Frontiers in Sustainable Cities, 5.* https://doi.org/10.3389/frsc.2023.1154464

Paabort, H., & Kõiv, K. (2022). Youth not in education, employment, or training: Practical reasons and support in Estonia. In Š. Bojnec & C. Petrescu (Eds.), *Youth policy application of the intervention: Best-practices with rural NEETs* (pp. 137–157). COST Action CA 18213.

Pearce, W., & Raman, S. (2014). The new Randomised Controlled Trials (RCT) movement in public policy: Challenges of epistemic governance. *Policy Sciences, 47*(4), 387–402. https://doi.org/10.1007/s11077-014-9208-3

Pedanik, R., Aps, J., Jaanits, J., Kostabi, E., & Kaasik, J. (2021). *A cross-sectoral model of cooperation on support and services for young people in NEET situations for local authorities.* Education and Youth Board.

Poštrak, M., Žalec, N., & Berc, G. (2020). Social integration of young persons at risk of dropping out of the education system: Results of the Slovenian programme project learning for young adults. *Revija Za Socijalnu Politiku, 27*(33), 287–308. https://doi.org/10.3935/rsp.v27i3.1740

Quintano, C., Mazzocchi, P., & Rocca, A. (2018). The determinants of Italian NEETs and the effects of the economic crisis. *Genus, 74*(1), 1–24. https://doi.org/10.1186/s41118-018-0031-0

Radin, B. (2019). *Policy analysis in the twenty-first century: Complexity, conflict, and cases.* Routledge & CRC Press.

Rhodes, R. (2019). Public administration, the interpretive turn and storytelling. In *A Research Agenda for Public Administration* (pp. 12–27). Edward Elgar.

Santos-Brien, R. (2018). *Effective outreach to NEETs. Experience from the ground.* European Commission.

Serracant, P. (2014). A brute indicator for a NEET case: Genesis and evolution of a Problematic concept and results from an alternative indicator. *Social Indicators Research, 117*(2), 401–419. https://doi.org/10.1007/s11205-013-0352-5

Simmons, R. (2017). Employability, knowledge and the creative arts: Reflections from an ethnographic study of NEET young people on an entry to employment programme. *Research in Post-Compulsory Education, 22*(1), 22–37. https://doi.org/10.1080/13596748.2016.1272086

Social Insurance Board. (2021). A cross-sectoral model of cooperation for local governments for supporting and providing services to young people in NEET status, adapted overview.

Stabingis, L. (2020). Impact of youth guarantee initiatives on NEETs population changes in EU. *Management Theory and Studies for Rural Business and Infrastructure Development, 42*, 145–156. https://doi.org/10.15544/mts.2020.15

Stone, D. A. (1997). *Policy paradox: The art of political decision making.* W.W. Norton.

Strecker, T., López, J., & Cabasés, M. À. (2021). Examining NEET situations in Spain: Labour market, discourses and policies. *Journal of Applied Youth Studies, 4*(2), 119–134. https://doi.org/10.1007/s43151-021-00048-2

Sucha, V., & Sienkiewicz, M. (2020). *Science for policy handbook.* Elsevier.

Thompson, R. (2011). Individualisation and social exclusion: The case of young people not in education, employment or training. *Oxford Review of Education, 37*(6), 785–802. https://doi.org/10.1080/03054985.2011.636507

Uman, L. S. (2011). Systematic reviews and meta-analyses. *Journal of the Canadian Academy of Child and Adolescent Psychiatry, 20*(1), 57–59.

Voorberg, W., Bekkers, V., & Tummers, L. (2013). Co-creation and co-production in social innovation: A systematic review and future research agenda. *Public Management. Review, 17*, 1333–1357. https://doi.org/10.1080/14719037.2014.930505

Wasserman, S., & Faust, K. (1994). *Social network analysis: Methods and applications.* Cambridge University Press.

Weimer, D. L., & Vining, A. R. (2017). *Policy analysis: Concepts and practice.* Routledge.

Windsor, D. (2017). Value creation theory: Literature review and theory assessment. *Stakeholders Management, 4*, 75–100. https://doi.org/10.1108/S2514-175920170000004

Zhartay, Z., Khussainova, Z., & Yessengeldin, B. (2020). Development of the youth entrepreneurship: Example of Kazakhstan. *Entrepreneurship and Sustainability Issues, 8*(1), 1190–1208. https://doi.org/10.9770/jesi.2020.8.1(80)

Open Access This chapter is licensed under the terms of the Creative Commons Attribution 4.0 International License (http://creativecommons.org/licenses/by/4.0/), which permits use, sharing, adaptation, distribution and reproduction in any medium or format, as long as you give appropriate credit to the original author(s) and the source, provide a link to the Creative Commons license and indicate if changes were made.

The images or other third party material in this chapter are included in the chapter's Creative Commons license, unless indicated otherwise in a credit line to the material. If material is not included in the chapter's Creative Commons license and your intended use is not permitted by statutory regulation or exceeds the permitted use, you will need to obtain permission directly from the copyright holder.

SPRINGER NATURE

GPSR Compliance

The European Union's (EU) General Product Safety Regulation (GPSR) is a set of rules that requires consumer products to be safe and our obligations to ensure this.

If you have any concerns about our products, you can contact us on ProductSafety@springernature.com

In case Publisher is established outside the EU, the EU authorized representative is:

Springer Nature Customer Service Center GmbH
Europaplatz 3
69115 Heidelberg, Germany

The manufacturer's authorised representative in the EU is Springer Nature Customer Service Centre GmbH, Europaplatz 3, 69115 Heidelberg, Germany. If you have any concerns regarding our products, please contact ProductSafety@springernature.com

Printed and bound by CPI Group (UK) Ltd, Croydon, CR0 4YY

25/03/2026

02078170-0011